Free Enterprise Urban Transportation

by
Gabriel Roth and George G. Wynne

Transaction Books
New Brunswick (U.S.A.) and London (U.K.)

Copyright © 1982 by the Council for International Urban Liaison, Washington, D.C. 20006

All rights reserved under International and Pan-American Copyright Conventions. No part of this book may be reproduced or transmitted in any form or by any means, electronic or mechanical, including photocopy, recording, or any information storage and retrieval system, without prior permission in writing from the publisher. All inquiries should be addressed to the Council for International Urban Liaison, Washington, D.C. 20006.

Library of Congress Catalog Number: 82-4739
ISBN: 0-87855-914-0 (paper)
Printed in the United States of America

Library of Congress Cataloging in Publication Data

Roth, Gabriel Joseph, 1926-
    Free enterprise urban transportation.

    1. Underdeveloped areas—Urban transportation.

2. Urban transportation. I. Wynne, George G.
II. Title.
HE305.R67   388.4'09172'4   82-4739
ISBN 0-87855-914-0   AACR2

No claim of copyright is entered for those portions of this book which are taken verbatim from material prepared with U.S. Government funds under contract UMTA-DC-06-0150. The findings are those of the authors and do not necessarily reflect the views or policy of the U.S. Department of Transportation, Urban Mass Transportation Administration. This publication does not constitute a standard, specification, or regulation.

Contents

Preface by Neal R. Peirce v

Chapter 1 Overview 1

Chapter 2 Examples of Financially Viable Urban Public
           Transportation Systems 7

Chapter 3 Characteristics of Successful Public Transportation
           Systems 29

Chapter 4 Application in the U.S.: Possibilities and Problems 39

Chapter 5 A Practical Implementation Program 59

Annex
          Source References 66
          Shared Ride Policy Statement 68
          Ordinances 69
          Index 71

Acknowledgments

Prophets are generally not honored in their own country. The paratransit prophets and practitioners are no exception. In the developed world they are barely taken seriously; in the developing nations where the market practices what they preach, they are ignored or at best tolerated because decision makers hanker after the big and costly systems that earn prestige but gobble up resources. The authors want to acknowledge first of all the support and encouragement of Jimmy Yu, an unsung poet of small informal urban transportation systems, whose work at the Urban Mass Transportation Administration has set in motion research initiatives all over the country and the world to find better ways of identifying and dealing with the urban mobility needs of the late 20th century. He and his colleagues have aided and made possible the work of researchers like Ron Kirby to whom we are indebted for the information on Cairo's jitneys. We also acknowledge that host of pioneers whose contributions are cited under our source references.

Our special thanks go to Dan Roos and Multisystems for supporting our research within the framework of his major paratransit study. We appreciate the comments of syndicated urban columnist Neal R. Peirce, who contributed the preface, Professor Clark Oglesby of the University of California, Anthony Shephard, who played a key role in introducing informal public transportation in Hong Kong and in Kuala Lumpur, and Ken Orski, founder of the Corporation for Urban Mobility, all of whom reviewed the text. A special expression of gratitude is reserved for the individuals and institutions too numerous to mention here who answered our queries and gave us access to their case studies, research and photographs. Pam Loos of the Council and Sonia Molina of the Economic Development Institute had an important role in readying the text for publication. They all share in whatever contribution the following pages can make in the search for alternatives to the costly, cumbersome and unprofitable monopolies that provide public transportation in our cities. For mistakes and omissions the authors alone are responsible.

Preface

No one who has ever ridden on the magnificent public transportation systems of a Paris or Toronto, a London or Hamburg would disparage the wonders of clean and efficient rapid rail systems interlocked with well-managed light rail and bus service. The city can be traversed quickly, inexpensively, safely; the service is dependable, the equipment a pleasure to ride in.

Sadly, however, practically all the public transit authorities of the United States are in deep trouble today. Seriously inflated labor costs, mounting deficits, equipment breakdowns and lagging ridership afflict a vast majority. Few, if any, seem to have a reasonable chance of rising to the level of one of the great international systems. Adulation of the private automobile, combined with a popular disdain for mass transit as a kind of publicly subsidized sop to the poor or aged, seems too deeply ingrained. The order of the day seems to be a vicious circle of fare increases, declining ridership and lower service levels which invite less public support and subsidy.

Yet as the authors of *Free Enterprise Urban Transportation* tell us, there is an alternative if we will shift our attention to some of the less developed nations of the world. In Africa, in Asia, in parts of Latin America, one finds flourishing, privately-owned, profitable modes of public transportation that are able to provide city residents with relatively fast, frequent and convenient service—and all that at highly affordable prices. Private public transportation takes many names, shapes and organizational forms from Argentina to Zaïre. It is characterized in many cases by fleets of collective taxis, jitneys and microbuses that cruise the streets and provide door-to-door or main line service. In the least developed countries, human-powered pedal cabs and motorized three-wheelers are also used. Sometimes these systems are only grudgingly tolerated by local authorities who are intent on projecting a modern, more prestigious image for their cities. But the alternative systems are a success story by all service criteria. Moreover, they provide substantial employment.

The secret, of course, is the entrepreneurial spirit. There is abundant evidence that a small, privately-run enterprise is inherently more efficient than a large monopoly sustained in large part by the taxpayer. Owner-operators work harder, handle more jobs and have less overhead than public enterprises protected by subsidies. Invariably the private operator has less capital and will opt for smaller vehicles—taxis, vans or microbuses—which in turn are cheaper to acquire, easier to fill and more economical to operate than standard-sized buses. Thus they turn a profit while charging their passengers competitive and sometimes lower fares than the publicly-owned systems.

The authors argue cogently that economy of scale does not favor the large bus or rail vehicle except at peak hours along corridors of maximum demand. Even there, they note, privately-owned jitneys and microbuses can take pressure off the peak and allow the public operator to save money by getting along with less costly big equipment.

This book is exciting reading: the case studies are fascinating themselves; collectively they represent a strong case for experimenting, soon and imaginatively, with alternative, free enterprise-sponsored transportation in the United States.

Neal R. Peirce

1
Overview

This report challenges the conventional wisdom that public transportation in cities cannot be provided at a profit, that it has to be supplied by publicly-owned or franchised monopolies, and that services have to be slow and costly. We will describe a number of public transportation systems abroad (largely, but not exclusively, in developing countries) that operate at a profit, and will indicate what could be done to enable the United States to develop networks of fast, reliable urban public transportation services responsive to users' needs, at prices that most can afford.

Following this overview, Chapter 2 gives examples of different types of urban public transportation that run at a profit while providing good service; Chapter 3 attempts to distill from the evidence the characteristics of successful urban public transportation systems; Chapter 4 reviews the private provision of public transportation in U.S. cities and considers the possibilities of its expansion; and Chapter 5 outlines how lessons from abroad might be applied in the United States.

Throughout the report, the term *public transportation* will be used to mean *transportation available to the public*. Whether systems are *publicly-owned* or *privately-owned*; whether they are trains, buses, minibuses, taxis or rickshaws; they will be covered by the generic heading *public transportation*.

Examples of Successful Public Transportation Systems

Minibuses in Hong Kong and Kuala Lumpur. Minibus services in Hong Kong and Kuala Lumpur were introduced to meet needs that the regular services would not satisfy. They have become extremely popular, with the result that the authorities currently limit their numbers to 4,350 in Hong Kong and 400 in Kuala Lumpur to protect the regular, franchised services. In consequence, the fortunate owners of licenses obtain substantial financial returns from their vehicles.

Route Associations in Buenos Aires and Calcutta. In some cities, individual bus owners form an association to operate a bus route. Each member of the association owns and operates his own bus, while the association has the responsibility of operating a particular route. These associations, which have to compete against other public transport buses, have rules to regularize the relationships between members: for example, buses have to keep to timetables so as not to "steal" customers from preceding and following buses. In the case of Buenos Aires, virtually all city buses are operated by route associations which compete against one another. (Buenos Aires is the only known example of a major city in which bus services were "demunicipalized" and returned to the private sector; the results are generally considered to have been a spectacular success.) In Calcutta, the private operators make enough profit to stay in business, while the public operating company, which charges the same fares and has similar routes, runs at a substantial deficit.

The Jeepneys of Manila. The Jeepney services, which were first operated by surplus U.S. Army jeeps (hence the name "Jeepneys"), offer an alternative service to that provided by the regular bus companies. Jeepneys are generally individually-owned, though many are organized in route associations. Fares are at similar levels to those of the regular bus companies, but while the regular bus companies are in financial difficulty, many of the operators of the 28,000 licensed Jeepneys are anxious to get more licenses to expand services.

The Dolmus of Istanbul, and the Minibuses of Cairo. Similar in principle to the Jeepneys, the Dolmus have been established in Turkey for many years. Cairo's minibuses, on the other hand, developed recently and rapidly in the light of official encouragement.

School Buses in Singapore. In Singapore, where school buildings are used for separate morning and afternoon shifts, and where neither shift coincides with business hours, school bus operators are empowered to enter into monthly contracts with office workers to take them from home to work on a regular basis. Casual pickup of workers is not allowed under this scheme, which gives each school bus operator six assured trips each day. There is, additionally, another supplementary service in Singapore, which allows private operators to ply for hire along designated routes, but only in peak periods.

The Matatu of Nairobi. These minibuses, similar in some way to those operating in Hong Kong and Kuala Lumpur, complement the services of the conventional bus company, and are particularly important in serving slum areas untouched by the regular service. The government of Kenya, with the help of the World Bank, is planning to establish a financing agency to finance the purchase of minibuses by private operators with a view to relieve urban unemployment and simultaneously to improve public transportation.

The Bakassi of Khartoum. The Bakassi, converted Toyota pickup trucks, carry tens of thousands of passengers per day. By mid-1979, 3,300 of them were operating on the crowded streets of Khartoum. Although Bakassi owners must contend with gas rations and short supplies of spare parts, the industry is thriving.

Shared Taxis in Belfast. "Black taxis" are operated by sectarian groups to enable their supporters to travel despite interruptions to the conventional services. They provide quick and low-cost transportation, under crowded conditions (up to eight people per shared taxi), but are profitable, though fares are no higher than those charged by the bus company.

The Publicos of Puerto Rico. Puerto Rico's "Publicos" (shared taxis and minibuses) have been established for many years as a service that offers higher speeds than the bus, at a higher fare. They have maintained their financial viability right into the 1980's, while the conventional bus system has been unable to cover its costs without subsidy.

Characteristics of Successful Public Transportation Systems

The systems described above, all of which are profitable, generally consist of small fleets of small vehicles and are often operated by small firms, on a competitive basis. The characteristics of these services may be summarized as follows:

Ownership. Almost without exception, ownership is private. Privately-owned firms, especially when subject to competition, tend to have lower costs than public agencies and to make more productive use of their resources.

Size of Firm. The successful transportation providers tend to be small firms, often owning one or two vehicles, reflecting the fact that there are few "economies of scale" in the provision of transportation. This allows management to have close control over vehicle operation and maintenance and over the disposal of the revenues.

Size of Vehicle. Many successful schemes use comparatively small vehicles—minibuses or shared taxis. This is often due to legal restrictions that prohibit the use of standard-sized buses by "informal" operators. However, despite the fact that small vehicles require more drivers, they have important advantages in low equipment costs and high speed.

Route Associations. Many successful operations involve a route association, whereby a number of private operators band together to run a route in common.

There are also problems with some of these successful services, which may be summarized as follows:

Unreliability. In the absence of a regulated supplier, public transportation users have no assurance that a particular service will be available when needed. A similar situation applies in the case of taxis in the U.S.

Anti-Social Driving Habits. As drivers of "informal" public transportation compete for passengers, they have been accused of racing one another, stopping in forbidden zones to pick up and set down passengers, and generally driving with disregard to the interests of other road users.

Neglect of Weak Routes. It has been suggested that if public transportation is provided only for profit, there will be no service on unprofitable routes. Chapter 3 addresses this objection and discusses how it can be overcome.

On balance, the disadvantages of free enterprise public transportation services can be corrected, and do not justify their discouragement in favor of franchised monopoly services, the general pattern in the U.S.

Application in the U.S.: Possibilities and Problems

Requirements of U.S. Urban Transportation Users. Travelers in U.S. cities seek transportation modes that offer characteristics such as high speed, low cost, comfort (e.g., a seat). There is evidence that the characteristic most sought after by travelers is *speed*. To most travelers, low cost is important, but speed is critical. It follows that, in order to be successful, a public transportation mode has to provide speed, the speed that matters being door-to-door speed.

The Likely Effect on Existing Transportation Services. Because existing services are burdened with having to provide costly peak-period services, with substantial use of equipment and labor that is idle outside the peak, they would stand to benefit from services that reduce peak demand. To the extent that competitive services were to draw away passengers in off-peak periods, the existing services would suffer. Drivers and other personnel employed full-time to provide only peak services would lose their jobs if the peak load were shifted to "informal" services. The hiring of part-time drivers represents a way of coping with this problem. However, local unions have resisted this practice vigorously in wage negotiations. Several U.S. cities, starting with San Diego and now including Washington, D.C., as well, have managed to overcome union objections and are employing part-time help for peak-period service.

The Effect of Competition on "Weak" Routes. The introduction of competitive services would tend to reduce or eliminate any monopoly profits earned by "strong" routes and reduce the possibility of such surpluses being used to subsidize "weak" routes. However, such "cross-subsidies" are unjustified by economics as well as by equity. If a community wishes to subsidize a particular group of travelers, e.g., school children or people living in a particular area, it can vote an explicit subsidy from general revenues. No logical case can be made for requiring the subsidy to be paid by the transportation operators or by travelers on other routes. If explicit subsidies were voted, the required services could be provided on a contract basis by small operators in the same way that school buses are operated in many cities. For example, Phoenix is saving several hundred thousand dollars a year by contracting out Sunday bus service to taxi operators instead of operating a bus fleet for a few hundred passengers. Between 300 and 400 passengers use the Sunday service at a subsidized fare that is slightly higher than the bus fare, but much less than a taxi fare. On a weekday, Phoenix's buses carry about 40,000 passengers.

U.S. Experience with "Informal" Public Transportation
Jitneys (shared private cars and taxis) operated successfully in many U.S. cities until prohibited by law. Some of these services still persist. *Shared Taxis* operate in Pittsburgh, Meriden, (Conn.) and a few other cities. This mode would have potential for substantial expansion, if there were an acceptable method of fare sharing that would benefit both the taxicab industry and its customers. *Subscription Services*, whereby passengers contract to travel on a regular basis by private bus or minibus, are a popular and growing mode of travel to work, as are *Van Pools*, which are similar to subscription services with the difference that the driving is done by one of the passengers. *Route Associations* of individual bus operators are found in New Jersey. They enable small family firms to provide route coverage at a profit.

A Practical Implementation Program
It is not suggested that all public transportation services in all U.S. cities could suddenly be provided, at a profit, by small operators. It is likely that in New York and in other large cities with corridors of heavy demand, informal services will play only an auxiliary role. However, there are many U.S. communities, including those with no bus or train services, where informal public transportation should be able to carry the whole load. The objective of policy clearly ought to be to encourage market forces to work where they can to produce better services, and to continue subsidies to selected, clearly-identified groups such as the disabled, senior citizens and school children. The following measures are called for:

Removal of regulatory obstacles. The powers of state and local authorities to franchise favored firms should be removed, and the public transportation field opened to all who can offer service in safe vehicles.

Abolition of control over fares. Fare fixing may be appropriate under conditions of monopoly franchises, but not when competition is allowed. Taxis could be required to display their fares without being required to have them approved by local officials.

Clarification of insurance arrangements. Small public transportation operators have difficulty in obtaining insurance, partly because of obscurities in the law. The law should be clarified, and insurance companies encouraged to provide protection at competitive rates.

Agreement on fare schedules for shared taxis. The potential for shared taxi services cannot be realized in the absence of fare schedules designed to benefit all concerned: the travelers and the taxi industry.

Private contracting. City authorities should, instead of operating transportation services themselves, contract the work by a process of bidding to private operators of buses, minibuses and taxis. A number of U.S. cities already recognize that private management of bus fleets is inherently more efficient than public management, though this recognition has not yet extended to allowing the operation of market forces in the actual provision of services. Private operation of public transportation services, possibly with management companies exercising an oversight role on behalf of the cities, ought to be the way to go.

In the early part of the century, transportation systems, whether publicly- or privately-operated, were productive and profitable because they catered to a heavy demand. The personal mobility brought by the private car has reduced the demand for public transportation to a fraction and shaped our cities and lifestyles to the point where we have little choice but to use personal motorized transport. As costs climb steeply and our roads are choked with traffic, yesterday's solution becomes today's problem. Once again we have a choice—to apply in the U.S. the lessons that have been applied successfully in many parts of the world. If we want high quality, profitable public transportation services in our cities, the remedies are in our hands.

2
Examples of Financially Viable Urban Public Transportation Systems

The Minibuses of Hong Kong
The five million people of Hong Kong, a thriving British colony, occupy an area of about 400 square miles on the south China coast. While the main populated parts of Hong Kong had been served by bus companies enjoying exclusive franchises since 1933, the existence throughout the Colony of illegal taxis (known as "Pak Pais") caused concern to the authorities. These vehicles were effectively used as small buses hired either by a group at an agreed rate for a specific journey or separately by a number of individuals who paid by the seat. In February 1960, the government allowed these vehicles to be licensed for the transportation of workers, school children, airline staff and hotel patrons. In 1961, it licensed Dual Purpose Vans to provide transportation for both freight and passengers. In addition to these legally registered vehicles, a considerable number of minibuses registered as private cars operated illegally for hire.

Although the government's policy favored the franchised services, on many routes their level and standard of service were so far below requirements that the traveling public was induced to use the non-franchised services. The number of vehicles offering such services is estimated to have more than tripled between 1961 and 1968.

During the political disturbances of 1967 when the franchised public transportation services were seriously disrupted by strikes, the illegal services effectively filled the void and became for a time an essential element of the Colony's transportation system. Their operations, which had previously been located in the comparatively remote areas near the Chinese border, were extended to the main centers of population. After the disturbances were over, the franchised services slowly recovered their pre-disturbance patronage and police action against illegal operators became more severe. Nevertheless, the popularity of the illegal services, particularly the minibuses which had played a major role in coping with travel demand dur-

TABLE 2.1

Characteristics	Maxicab	P.L.B.
Route structure	Routes fixed by authority as feeder services, avoiding major bus corridors.	No fixed routes, PLBs go along busy streets where customers can be picked up easily.
Fare	Fares fixed by authority according to a scale based on mileage. No differential between peak and off-peak periods.	No fixed fares. Often a high price is charged in the a.m. and p.m. peaks and a low fare (sometimes lower than buses) during slack periods.
Timetable	Timetables detailing hours of operation and frequency of service laid down by the authority.	No fixed timetable. Driver may cease service at any time. Sometimes operate late at night for much higher fares.
Form of Ownership	The whole fleet under central control and staffed by regular drivers.	Varied. There are owner-drivers; vehicles on rent to drivers; and salaried drivers.
Maintenance Facilities	Required to provide garage maintenance and depot facilities.	Maintenance by contracting with garages. Usually park overnight at PLB stands.
Restriction	Fixed routes authorized by authority. "Maxicabs" are allowed to set down passengers in some busy main streets.	Most of the busy main streets have some form of PLB restriction.

ing the disturbances, continued and increased. It was clear that a considerable proportion of the public preferred this mode of travel and was prepared to pay for the higher level of comfort and convenience that it offered.

After considerable deliberation, the government decided to legalize the minibus as a form of public transport and, in 1969, the *Public Light Bus* (PLB) was introduced as a legal form of public transportation. It proved so popular that by 1972 it was carrying a quarter of all public transport trips and by 1976 one third. By then the number of PLBs had reached 4,350, and the government, concerned about their effects on the franchised services, froze the number of licenses at that level.

The success of the PLBs was reflected in their profitability to their owners. In 1972, a government study estimated that owners would recoup their outlay within one year, and revised calculations made in 1980 estimated that two thirds of the purchase price of a vehicle would be recovered in one year. Not an unacceptable rate of return, even for Hong Kong!

The PLBs were, however, criticized for congregating on major routes and causing congestion there. Some transport planners argued that they should be banned from major corridors and relegated to the provision of "feeder" service to the franchised bus companies. These criticisms posed a dilemma for the Hong Kong government which, in essence, had to choose between consumer sovereignty and planner sovereignty. By their patronage, the consumers demonstrated their preference for the more comfortable PLBs on which all passengers had seats. The government attempted to resolve the problem by introducing "maxicabs" which can be described as "franchised PLBs." The differences between these services are summarized in Table 2.1.

By the end of 1980 there were 328 maxicabs operating in Hong Kong on a total of 53 routes, compared to over 4,000 PLBs. The government endeavored to further expand the maxicab network and to encourage ordinary PLBs to join the scheme. It is outside the scope of this report to pursue the questions raised by Hong Kong's policy toward the PLBs. Suffice it to say that they are an effective and financially viable form of public transportation which receives strong support from their customers despite the doubts of the professional transport planners. The taxi business, incidentally, also does well in Hong Kong. The fleet expands at the rate of 1,200 a year, and 9,834 vehicles were licensed at the end of 1980. New licenses, which are allocated at government auctions, fetch the equivalent of almost US$50,000. Most taxis are operated as family businesses.

The Minibuses of Kuala Lumpur

Kuala Lumpur, the capital of Malaysia, is a rapidly expanding urban area with a population of about one million. Public transportation service has been traditionally provided by eight private companies, each franchised to operate over a specific sector in the area. In the early 1970's, the authorities were concerned by the deterioration of the public transportation system and the rapid rate of private motorization associated with it. The problem facing Kuala Lumpur was one with which many city managements are familiar: the franchises granted to the private bus companies enabled them to provide a service which was considered adequate in the 1950's and 1960's and for which the companies received revenues which were then considered fair. However, the spread of private car ownership led to declines in bus speeds, service standards, ridership and profitability. The government was reluctant to allow the bus companies to raise fares because of the effect on living costs and it was also concerned that, even if permission were given, the bus companies might not improve their services. The possibility of taking the buses into public ownership was considered but was not an attractive alternative; the government suspected that this would create as many problems as it would solve.

Malaysians were familiar with the "informal" public transportation services provided in other cities in southeast Asia and decided to introduce such services in Kuala Lumpur. They invited Anthony Shephard, who had been Transport Commissioner in Hong Kong when the Public Light Buses were introduced there, to design a scheme for Kuala Lumpur. He recommended that applicants for licenses to run services along specific long-distance routes be invited. To encourage the minibuses to be used for long trips, he recommended that they charge a flat fare of M40¢ (US16¢) compared to the M5¢ (US2¢) per mile charged by the conventional bus services.

The scheme was introduced as part of an urban transportation project supported by the World Bank. The World Bank favored the introduction of the minibuses although its funds were not required to finance them: the operators were able to tap other sources of finance. Over 2,000 applications were received in response to the government's invitation. By the end of 1975 there were about 100 minibuses plying routes in the city; by October 1976 the number had risen to 320 and by 1978 to 400, at which level the number was frozen. As a result, the minibus service, which was conceived as a luxury service for long-distance commuters, became degraded by overcrowding and standing passengers. The ratios of load to capacity (based on 58 seated passengers for a conventional bus and 16 for a minibus) were 68% in the morning and 78% in the evening peak periods for conventional buses and 114% and 125%, respectively, for the minibuses.

Another consequence of the scarcity of minibuses was their profitability. Transportation experts in Malaysia estimated the annual return on investment for an operator who had a license at 37% (the return was lower for operators who had to rent their vehicles, or their licenses, or both). Another characteristic of the minibus, referred to earlier, is its relatively high occupancy rate compared to the conventional bus. Surveys carried out in 1978 indicated that in peak periods the minibus accounted for 35% of all bus trips to the central area, and 53% of the passenger miles (the percentage of passenger miles accounted for was higher than the percentage of trips because the average trip length by conventional bus was 2.4 miles compared to 5.1 miles by minibus). Thus, a fleet of 400 16-seat minibuses "produced" more passenger miles than did the 600 58-seat conventional buses that were estimated to have been operating at the time.

It might be asked why, given the pressure on the minibuses, the government did not issue more licenses. One of the reasons for this was that the minibuses were taking traffic from the conventional buses, and the authorities were reluctant to license more minibus capacity when there were under-utilized, full-sized buses. As in Hong Kong, the government had to choose between "consumer sovereignty" and "planner sovereignty." The fact that it had difficulty in coming down fairly and squarely on the side of the consumer does not alter the fact that the minibuses in Kuala Lumpur, as in Hong Kong, were, and are, financially viable by any standard.

Private Buses in Buenos Aires

Buenos Aires, the capital of Argentina, has a population of 9 million living in an area exceeding 1,500 square miles. It has a variety of transport modes, the most important being the "micro-bus" (or "colectivo" in the local jargon) which accounts for 54% of all trips and 75% of public transport trips.

The colectivos were developed in the 1920's when, as a result of a general economic crisis, many people could not afford to take taxis on their own. These vehicles were therefore used by groups of passengers; fares were paid by each passenger individually. These taxis ran on fixed routes which were chosen by the taxi drivers themselves. The shared taxi quickly showed certain virtues of its own and was favorably received by the general public because it offered more flexibility, higher speeds and greater frequencies than the underground and electric tramways. The colectivo vehicle developed from a 7-seater to an 11-seater; subsequently it grew to 14 and 17 seats, finally reaching 23 seats which is the typical unit providing service today.

TABLE 2.2
Estimated Costs, Revenues and Profits of Kuala Lumpur Minibuses[a]

Costs(M$)[b]		
1. Wages[c]	19,800	
2. Depreciation[d]	6,000	
3. Fuel	7,500	
4. Repair	7,500	
5. Office	1,000	
6. Tax	1,440	
7. Insurance	1,800	
Total Costs	45,040	
Revenues		
8. Fares	58,500	(US$27,200)
Total Revenues	58,500	
Profit	13,460	(US$6,300)

Annual Return on $36,000 minibus: 37%

Notes:
 a. Average figures derived from interviews by government staff during 1978.
 b. All costs in M$ 1$US = M$2.15
 c. Wages: driver $350/month and conductor $300/month; 2 shift operation, no wages for inspectors.
 d. Depreciation: a 6-year life for a $36,000 vehicle and a 5-year life for a $30,000 vehicle give the same annual depreciation of $6,000.

The micro-buses offered stiff competition to the tramways and underground systems and this caused the government to establish, in 1936, a "Corporate Enterprise" which was supposed to have had a total monopoly in supplying the city with public transportation services. Nevertheless, several micro-bus lines remained in existence until 1951, when a national enterprise known as "Transportes de Buenos Aires" took charge of all the services, including those of the "Corporate Enterprise."

However, the service operated by the "Transportes de Buenos Aires" deteriorated rapidly both in quality and financially. By 1959, it was losing the equivalent of US$1,200,000 per year. In 1962, the situation became intolerable and "Transportes de Buenos Aires" was dissolved. All the transportation services, except for the underground railway, were turned over to private companies. The trams and trolleybuses were dropped out of service and were replaced by regular full-sized buses. It is significant, however, that many of these were subsequently replaced by the 23-seat micro-buses.

The micro-buses still operate profitably and provide a level of service that is praised by all visitors to Buenos Aires. The organizational unit of the service is the route association ("Empresa"), which is an association of owner-drivers empowered to serve just one route. The owners joining an Empresa have to abide by its rules, which govern such matters as schedules and fares.

The Empresa is the formal employer of the drivers and assumes all the responsibility arising from the labor laws. The vehicle owners choose and replace the drivers and pay the operating expenditures of the vehicle. The income goes to the vehicle owners who either turn it over to a common fund for distribution among members of the Empresa, prorate it according with the mileage run by each vehicle or divide it through any other method that the Empresa may choose.

Each month the Empresa charges each of its members for a share of the administrative expenditures corresponding to each vehicle, the salaries paid, goods and services supplied for maintenance and, in the event that the company is financing the purchase of a vehicle, an installment payment.

The investments in vehicles and in repair facilities are part of the company's capital. A successful operation results in an increase in the value of its shares which cannot, however, be sold in the free market. Any disputes within an Empresa are settled at a members meeting. Each vehicle is generally entitled to one vote. One of the typical characteristics of the Empresa is the large number of members: although a member can own several vehicles or several members can own one vehicle, on average there is one partner per vehicle. About one third of the members work as drivers of their own vehicles.

The Empresas offer several advantages: each member is directly responsible for the operation of the unit he is in charge of, and he, aided by his family, does much of the work required to run and maintain the vehicle. The public benefits from the competition that occurs between different Empresas. New Empresas can be formed with the permission of the authorities. Labor productivity is high: on average, each micro-bus employs three persons to drive, maintain and repair it. Each vehicle produces 1.3 to 1.6 million passenger miles per year so average labor productivity is around 480,000 passenger miles per year per person employed. The total fleet is composed of 13,000 micro-buses; on average, 60 micro-buses are used on each route, about four per route mile.

The micro-buses in Buenos Aires are regulated by the Ministry of Public Works and Services (MOSP) which fixes fares and minimum frequencies for individual routes and governs the formation of new Empresas.

Private Buses in Calcutta
One of the largest, most densely populated and poorest cities in the world, Calcutta, supports a population of some 10 million in an area of fewer than 600 square miles. Private buses first appeared in the city toward the end of the 19th century but were banned in 1960 when all bus services were vested in the Calcutta State Transport Corporation (CSTC). The CSTC suffered from managerial and financial problems and, in 1966, was paralyzed by strikes. In response to public demand before the 1966 elections and to its need for ready cash, the government of West Bengal sold permits which enabled 300 private buses to be operated. These operated at a profit, although they charged the same fare (equivalent to about US½¢ per mile) as the money-losing CSTC, and though they had inferior routes. By the late 1970s, some 1,500 full-sized private buses were operating in Calcutta, in addition to about 500 private minibuses. Today, the private buses account for about two-thirds of all bus trips in Calcutta *without subsidy*. Meanwhile, the CSTC, which operates similar routes at the same fares, has to be subsidized to the equivalent of US$1 million a month by a government that is desperately short of funds for other purposes.

The success of the private bus operators has been attributed to three factors:

- *Keeping Vehicles on the Road.* As soon as a private bus breaks down it is repaired, often on the road, with needed parts, if necessary, being bought on the "black market." The CSTC, in contrast, has to go through "channels" to obtain spare parts and only half of its buses are generally on the road.
- *Fare Collection.* The private bus crews (who are paid a percentage of the revenues) make greater efforts to collect the fares than CSTC employees.

"Fare evasion" is estimated to be 25% on CSTC buses and negligible on private buses.
- *Higher Labor Productivity*. The State Corporation's staffing levels, at 30 employees per bus (1980), is one of the highest in the world.

A key factor in the success of the private buses in Calcutta is the route association. These associations—generally one for each route—were formed voluntarily and spontaneously by the private owners. Each owner retains control over the operation and maintenance of his vehicle and receives the fares collected on it. The associations have rules to govern relationships between the members: for example, vehicles have to run on time. This is important because a bus running late tends to pick up more than its "fair share" of passengers, at the expense of the following bus. Owners of buses which do not keep to time are fined, the fine money is distributed among the other members. It has been reported that the fines are, in some instances, proportional to the delay, at a specified rate per minute, and paid directly to the owner of the following bus.

The private bus operators in Calcutta vividly illustrate the proposition that, given a suitable organizational framework, privately-operated buses can provide and expand transportation services without subsidy while a municipal monopoly is unable to do so.

The Jeepneys of Manila

The predominant public transport carrier in Manila is the Jeepney, which has become the Filipinos' favorite form of urban transport. Their fondness for this unique vehicle is rooted in the fact that it was invented in the aftermath of World War II when the city of Manila was just beginning its recovery from wartime devastation and neglect. The Jeepney was made from—and named after—the U.S. Army jeep. The chassis was extended and its back portion opened and adjusted to provide a central entry and exit. The roof was curved on all sides with prominent overhangs at the back. Two upholstered benches were attached lengthwise to accommodate the passengers. Thus the Jeepney became a symbol of the Filipinos' indomitability in times of crisis and of their capacity to survive. The Jeepneys also nurtured Filipino ingenuity and craftsmanship as they underwent various renovations and improvements. They are locally manufactured with the bodies made of sheet steel, some gaily painted with various decorations providing a wide variety of color and design.

According to figures compiled by the Manila Board of Transportation, there are about 28,000 Jeepneys in Manila (unofficial estimates put the figure at 60,000), compared to 2,900 buses. Jeepneys are a major form of transportation in Manila, accounting for about half of total trips while buses and private cars (including taxis) account for about 25% each.

One of Manila's gaudy "Jeepneys"

Loading through the rear door

TABLE 2.3
Manila Bus and Jeepney Costs
(1976 U.S. cents)

	Cost/Mile		Cost/Seat Mile	
Cost Item	**Bus***	**Jeepney***	**Bus***	**Jeepney***
Depreciation	7.4[a]	0.75	0.128	0.054[a]
Interest	4.9	0.55	0.084	0.039
Maintenance	6.7[b]	0.85	0.116	0.061
Tires	2.16	0.476	0.037	0.034
Fuel	5.5	4.48	0.095	0.32
Oil	0.384	0.17	0.007	0.012
Wages	9.6[c]	3.4	0.166	0.243
Management	0.44[d]	—	0.008	—
Total	37.08	10.68	.641	0.763
Total excluding wages	27.48	7.27	0.475	0.519
Total Operating Costs	24.34	9.376	0.420	0.67
(fuel tax)	(0.55)	(1.70)	(0.01)	(0.12)
Adjustments: (factor cost of fuel)	(4.95)	(2.78)	(0.086)	(0.20)
Total Excluding Wages (after adjustment to exclude fuel tax)	26.93	5.58	0.465	0.40

Notes:

* Bus: 58 seats; Jeepney: 14 seats.

a. Depreciation estimates are based on a capital cost of US$30,666 for a 55-seat stage bus with an expected 10-year life. The Jeepney costs US$2,972 for a 14-seat vehicle lasting on average 7.5 years. Buses average 46,500 miles/year; Jeepneys 50,000 miles. It is worth noting that the capital cost per seat mile of a bus is about 2½ times that of a Jeepney. 75% of depreciation cost is treated as dependent on the distance traveled, with the remaining 25% determined by time in use.

b. Maintenance costs for the two vehicle types are proportionate: 300 hours of labor time, and parts cost estimated at 10% of vehicle cost.

c. Wage costs of Jeepneys and bus differ in wage rates paid and size of crew employed. A bus operates with a driver (@P 5/hr.) and conductor (@P 4/hr.) Jeepneys employ only a driver @P 2.5/hr.

d. License and insurance costs are not provided.

Source: A.A. Walters, "Costs and Scale of Bus Services." World Bank Staff Working Paper No. 325, World Bank, Washington, D.C., 1979.

The enterprising Jeepney operators provide living proof that even the unskilled and poorly educated can succeed through initiative, hard work and calculated risk-taking. As an employment medium, the Jeepney industry in Manila alone gives direct employment to over 100,000 people. This includes 2-3 drivers for each of the 28,000 vehicles, about 10,000 Jeepney operators and several thousand more who are involved in servicing the vehicles and building bodies for them. In addition, it is estimated that a further

400,000 depend for their livelihoods in one way or the other on the Jeepney industry. There are, for instance, manufacturers of Jeepney cassette radios, plastic ornaments, seat upholstery; and trip dispatchers at Jeepney terminals.

Since their inception, the Jeepneys have provided stiff competition to the regular buses, and the representatives of each mode regularly call for the suppression of the other. Transportation experts have long disputed the relative merits of Jeepneys and buses in Manila, where their operations almost completely overlap. The fares are also the same, and they are equally acceptable socially. Buses are perceived by some to be more comfortable for longer journeys, while Jeepneys are the more agile and therefore faster for short runs. Within recent years the conventional buses have had difficulty in maintaining their services, while Jeepney operators have been agitating for more licenses and operating illegally. This suggests that the Jeepneys are the more cost effective form of transport, and this is borne out by the published figures of comparative costs of the two modes, tabulated in Table 2.3, which show the costs of a 14-seat Jeepney are about a quarter of the costs of a 58-seat bus.

The transportation policymakers in the Philippines have, since 1976, been engaged in an attempt to rationalize the urban transportation system in favor of conventional buses which they consider to be more cost-effective and fuel-efficient than the Jeepneys. However, the authorities have no way of replacing the Jeepneys without massive public investments in transport which they are reluctant to undertake; the national leadership is also unwilling to deprive the tens of thousands of Filipino Jeepney owners and drivers and their families of their primary source of income. The government therefore decided to "freeze" the size of the Jeepney fleet and to discourage Jeepney use on main roads. "Instead of loitering over the main city roads," declared a senior government official, "Jeepneys will now be concentrated on complementary, secondary or feeder routes where they will virtually act as primary linkages or conveyor belts between residential areas and certain business districts." This is not the place to discuss transport policy in Manila. Suffice it to say that the development of the Filipino Jeepney industry provides further evidence that public transportation can operate profitably and successfully in a large metropolitan area.

The Dolmus/Minibus System in Istanbul

Massive migration from rural areas to major urban centers in Turkey has created complex problems of urban living that have strained the capacity of the local authorities to provide even the most essential public services. One feature of this general problem has been the failure of the municipal bus and other government-operated public transportation systems to meet the routine travel needs of people. As a result of this situation, the Dolmus/minibus system has emerged as an indigenous form of public transportation in Istanbul. Today, over one-half of the daily travel needs of the public is served by the Dolmus (4-5 passenger cars that can operate either as sole-use taxis or as shared taxis), and 12-seater minibuses. In Istanbul there are currently about 16,000 Dolmus (the word "Dolmus," which means "stuffed," is used both in the singular and the plural, like "sheep") and about 4,000 minibuses.

Istanbul traffic options are not as simple as they might appear on the surface and the Dolmus/minibuses can provide a panoply of services:

Dolmus only. Service along fixed routes is provided by some 7-seater station wagons, but mostly by 5-seater vehicles distinguished by a continuous yellow band around the vehicle and/or the "Dolmus" sign placed or written on the vehicle.

Dolmus/taxi. For this kind of operation, mostly conducted in 5-passenger vehicles, the operator may switch from Dolmus operation to sole-use taxi operation either instantly (when congestion and demand levels are high) or on some days when he prefers to operate as a taxi.

Taxi/Dolmus. This is also a mixed operation of 5-passenger vehicles mainly used as taxis and occasionally as Dolmus.

Taxi/on-the-way-back-Dolmus. This type of operation is self-explanatory; a taxi operates as a Dolmus on the return trip to the driver's home or to his usual taxi queue. (Demands for this kind of service were recently made by London taxi drivers and users.)

Taxi. A conventional taxi service is provided generally in 4-passenger or 5-passenger vehicles.

Minibus. An operation along a fixed route is generally carried out in minibuses seating 9 or 10 passengers.

Midibus. The vehicle is used as a minibus, but has a capacity of 13 or more passengers.

There are also variations on these categories, such as the "express Dolmus" provided when demand is high, at twice the regular fare (a practice resented by the traveling public); "shared taxi" whereby a number of passengers in the waiting line share a taxi to the same destination; and unlicensed Dolmus service provided by private passenger cars. Some private cars also operate illegally as taxicabs, a practice not unknown in New York. In peak periods the minibuses and midibuses tend to be severely overloaded, which adds significantly to the profits of the operators and to the discomfort of the passengers. Needless to say, this overloading is associated with a restriction on the number of minibus licenses and the consequent power of the operators to obtain "abnormal" profits.

The situation of public transportation in Istanbul cannot be described as a happy one. The buses operated by the franchised company are overcrowded and run at a large financial loss. The Dolmus and minibuses provide profitable services but some members of the public resent being "taken for a ride." Finally, private car users also object to the Dolmus on the ground that they take up valuable road space—though Dolmus use much less space per passenger than do the private cars. Nevertheless, there can be no doubt that the Dolmus and minibuses of Istanbul are successful business enterprises and financially viable.

Taxis and Jitneys in Cairo

Cairo, the largest urban center in the Middle East, has a population of 8 ½ million spread over an area of 800 square miles. It suffers from severe traffic congestion and a heavily overloaded network of bus and tram services. In recent years the transportation system was substantially improved by the development of privately-owned shared taxis and jitney services.

Metered taxis in Cairo provided two distinct kinds of service: exclusive service for which one or more passengers are carried directly from origin to destination, and (illegal) shared service for which the driver may stop along the route to pick up or drop off passengers without obtaining the permission of other passengers in the taxi. The price for the exclusive service is typically negotiated at a rate which (at least for tourists) is substantially above the metered rate. The price for shared trips, on the other hand, is typically based on the meter. These services appear to work quite well though there are ambiguities about the fare levels. There are also a substantial number of unmetered taxis in Cairo, some of which are inter-city taxis operating illegally. The existence of these taxis suggests that the number officially licensed for public service is insufficient, which is strange, as there are no restrictions on the number of taxis that may be licensed.

Fixed-route jitney services were allowed to operate in the late 1970s. As is usual in the Middle East, vehicles normally wait until they have a full load and then leave the terminal, rather than leaving at fixed intervals and keeping a few seats available for passengers along the route. (A similar system is operated in Amman, and by the "Sherut" shared inter-city taxis in Israel.) Passengers are only able to join the jitneys at mid-route when the vehicles stop to drop passengers off. A survey in 1979 established that there were about 800 vehicles participating in the scheme, running at intervals of 3-5 minutes. The system expanded rapidly in that year and the maximum legal seating capacity of the vehicles was raised from 12 to 15 seats.

A union of taxi drivers and minibus operators runs the scheme. It carries out a variety of services, including the organization of new routes and the determination of the fares to be charged. The union also employs and pays dispatchers from a 5% ticket tax collected by the dispatchers at the terminals. The dispatchers receive a fixed salary plus a bonus if they collect more than a certain amount of money per day. The ticket tax is also used to finance the construction of signs and waiting facilities at jitney terminals. The union representatives claim that demand exists for at least 2,000 vehicles and that the service can be substantially expanded.

The most sought-after vehicle is the locally-assembled "Ramses" minibus. It owes its popularity not only to its comparatively low cost ($7,000 compared to $12,000 for a VW or Mazda vehicle of the same capacity), but also to its powerful engine and its durability under Cairo driving conditions. Eighty percent of new vehicles are said to be owned by persons outside the taxicab industry who lease vehicles to drivers for 25% of their fare collections. Many investors own over 4 vehicles. About 20% of vehicles are driven by owners. Minibus fares are 3-4 times the regular Cairo bus fare, which is equivalent to US5¢. Much of the repair and maintenance is done by the drivers themselves in small workshops.

Cairo's conventional bus and tram services do not cover their costs, and are subsidized to the equivalent of over $50 million a year. The rapid growth of high-quality "informal" systems provides yet another illustration of the willingness of travelers to pay for improved service and of the ability of the private sector to provide, at a profit, services for which the public sector chalks up deficits.

There are also special express ("limousine") taxi services to and from the airport. The charges are fixed according to destination. One company alone operates about 500 of these vehicles.

Supplementary Bus Services of Singapore

In November 1973, the government of Singapore, a city-state with a population of 2.2 million people living in an area of 227 square miles, concerned about increasing automobile ownership and traffic congestion, took a number of radical measures to improve public transportation. One measure was the unification of the main bus companies into the newly formed Singapore Bus Service (SBS), Ltd. Nevertheless, public transport services were still considered to be inadequate, so the Supplementary Public Transport Service (SBTS) Schemes A and B were introduced in March 1974.

Scheme A. Scheme A was introduced to cater to adult office and factory workers. Under this scheme, trucks, delivery vehicles, and school buses are permitted to transport workers between their homes and places of work. By June 1981, a total of 2,169 vehicles had been issued with Scheme A permits, comprising 191 trucks, 379 private hire buses and 1,599 school buses. Under Scheme A there is no restriction on the operating hours but it is not permitted to pick up individual travelers on public roads. Payment can only be by monthly contract, at rates freely negotiated between the operators and their passengers. To appreciate the effectiveness of this scheme, readers should be aware that schools in Singapore operate on a double shift system,

One of Singapore's privately-owned and profitable supplementary services

some children going to school in the morning and others in the afternoon. Furthermore, the beginning and end of the school hours are different from the beginning and end of business hours, so that the school bus operator with a Scheme A permit is able to make six trips a day: two round trips for school children and one round trip for adult workers.

Scheme B. Scheme B was introduced to cater to peak-hour demand for public bus transport. By June 1981, 27 designated routes were operating between housing centers and the central business district (CBD) and 19 routes between housing centers and industrial areas. As of June 30, 1981, a total of 610 vehicles were licensed under Scheme B, 395 of them school buses. Under Scheme B, vehicles are allowed to pick up and set down passengers at authorized stopping points, but only during the morning and evening peak periods, which are typically 6 a.m. to 9:45 a.m. and 4:15 p.m. to 7:30 p.m.

Scheme A proved to be more popular with operators than Scheme B; in February 1980, over 80% of vehicles licensed under Scheme A were operating, while only 66% of Scheme B. The lower popularity of Scheme B has been attributed to its less profitable operation, which stemmed from shorter operating hours and longer waiting periods at starting points.

While these supplementary services in Singapore carry a significant number of passengers—about 144,000 trips a day—their contribution is small compared to that of the SBS fleet, which carries over 2.2 million. There are other supplementary bus services in Singapore in addition to those described above: the City Shuttle Service, the Singapore Airport Bus Service, and the Air-conditioned Coach Services, which operate only in peak hours on working days and are designed to attract the car commuter by providing a high-quality bus service. All the supplementary services operate at a profit.

The Matatu of Nairobi
Nairobi (population 736,000), the bustling capital of Kenya, is known, among other things, for its heavy traffic congestion in the weekday peak periods. It is also the home of an informal public transportation vehicle known as the Matatu which appears in several forms:

- Light pick-up vehicles seating 12-14 passengers.
- Minibuses, seating 15 passengers (VW Kombis) or 18 (Nissan E20 with long wheel base).
- Large pick-ups, seating 14-24 passengers.
- Midibuses, seating 25 passengers.

In 1979, 1,550 privately-operated Matatu were counted, carrying 66,000 passengers daily. The Matatu travel all over Nairobi, along bus routes and along narrow roads which the buses do not penetrate, and they are often overloaded well beyond their payload capacity, i.e. the 15-passenger VW Kombi has a "crush" passenger capacity of 20. Some Matatu operate only part-time. Some are company cars which, reportedly, carry passengers in peak periods without the owners' knowledge. Others, particularly the pick-ups, have fold-up seats and are used for carrying goods as well as passengers. Some of the vehicles are in very poor condition and are maintained only to the extent necessary to keep them running.

The majority of owners have a single vehicle; about 40% of Matatu are reported to be owner-driven. Some owners have two vehicles, driving one and employing a driver for the other. Where a driver is employed, the most common owner-driver relationship is for the driver to pay the owner a fixed sum each day, and use the remainder of the collections for gasoline, minor repairs and compensation for himself and the conductor. (This agreement is common in some U.S. cities between taxi owners and taxi drivers.) In some cases the owner pays the driver a fixed monthly wage.

As the demand for transport in Kenya is acute, Matatu owners seem to have no problem in finding lucrative routes. The profits enable vehicles to be paid off in two years, and can then be reinvested in other vehicles or other ventures. A number of owners are known to have bought farms on the proceeds. The most successful operators own over 15 minibuses plying in Nairobi and on several inter-city routes.

The franchised bus company in Nairobi has protested the activities of the Matatu, but it does not protest too strongly as it does not have the capacity to meet full peak demand for public transportation. The authorities in Kenya recognize the importance of Matatu operations—both to travelers and to operators—but are concerned about their safety. The Matatu have a reputation for being dangerous (the light pick-ups being particularly deadly when they roll over), although there is no firm evidence that they are more dangerous than other vehicles in Kenya. The authorities are trying, with the assistance of the World Bank, to improve the Matatu service by enforcing safety and insurance requirements, providing convenient maintenance facilities, and guaranteeing a loan fund to enable low-income people to buy Matatu.

The Bakassi of Khartoum

The single bright spot in the public transportation scene of Khartoum (population 1.6 million) is provided by the Bakassi, the Sudan's version of the Matatu, that carry tens of thousands of passengers daily. Non-existent in 1973, their number grew to 3,300 in mid-1979 when a ban on further licenses was imposed by the local authorities because of the part the vehicles play in the bustling capital's perennial traffic jam. The Bakassi have been accused of adding to the chaos in the streets because they take on and discharge passengers anywhere. They have no fixed stops and parking places, which adds to their appeal from the public's point of view, but they employ under-age boys as fare collectors and hawkers. Accidents involving the children have tarnished the Bakassi owners' image with the authorities and the traveling public. Yet they are a thriving industry despite all sorts of strictures including a daily gas ration, totaling a mere five gallons, forcing owners to buy fuel on the black market. Bakassi are banned from several squares in the center of the city and they have trouble getting spare parts which are in perennial short supply and must be bought under the table at exorbitant prices.

The Bakassi sprang up as a free market answer to steadily deteriorating city bus service. Less than 140 of the public bus company's fleet of about 450 Mercedes and Magirus Deutz buses are in operation because of the spare part problem. The remaining buses have to cover a network of 46 lines which means hours of waiting and intolerably crowded conditions unless one of the speedy, privately-operated *Boks* can be hailed. The box-like appearance of the Bakassi is responsible for that nickname.

The publicly-owned Capital Transport Company currently employs a staff of about 1,400 or about 10 people including maintenance and management personnel for each bus now on the road—a huge deficit operation. A consortium of businessmen reportedly is planning to import and operate 200 micro-buses to cope with and profit from the mobility needs of the capital's expanding population.

Catching a Matatu in Nairobi presents a challenge

The family-run "Publicos" of Puerto Rico have been handling a major share of the traffic load for 25 years

Shared Taxis in Belfast

To counter the argument that profit-making urban transportation can work only in developing countries, one can cite the "black taxis" of Belfast, which emerged in the early 1970's following disruption of conventional bus service by civil disturbances. These vehicles (called "black taxis" because they are actually ex-London taxis, most of which are black) appeared first in Catholic working class areas of Belfast and later also in Protestant areas. Although the taxis are normally operated by owner-drivers, they are regulated by local taxi-owner associations which limit the number of taxis operating in their areas of influence and decide who operates them and under what conditions. By 1977, the total number of taxis operating was estimated to range between 500 and 600.

The black taxis operate a high-frequency shared taxi service at relatively high speeds. Passengers are picked up or set down along fixed routes between the city center and the particular areas served. Dispatchers are employed at the city end to organize passengers into taxi loads for different destinations in order to speed up the system. Fares are fixed and, what is perhaps most surprising to transportation experts, are generally lower than those offered by the regular city bus service. On the other hand comfort standards are low, with as many as 8 adults in each vehicle at peak periods. But, in general, the consensus in Belfast is that the service provided by the black taxis represents an efficient and economical form of public transport. This is reflected in their patronage which, on weekdays, is estimated to cover about 50% of all public transport trips on the main routes served by them. The key to the financial success of the black taxis seems to be their relatively high load factor. This is believed to have ranged from 43% to 82% in 1974, compared to bus load factors which ranged from 15% to 46%.

Four main criticisms are leveled at the black taxi operators:

First, the full costs of maintenance and insurance are not paid. Safety standards are enforced by the taxi associations themselves, but there have been problems with insurance, stemming from the fact that the insurance companies are generally unwilling to insure the black taxis other than as private cars.

Second, the drivers have been accused of competing aggressively for passengers, of overloading, of selfish driving behavior (parking in restricted zones to pick up or drop off passengers, of making U-turns, etc.). Such complaints against taxi drivers are not uncommon in other cities.

Third, the services have been criticized on the grounds that the conventional bus services are faced with unfair competition; unfair because the publicly-owned bus company has to meet uneconomic social obligations, such as providing services at peak periods and late at night, when costs cannot be covered by revenues. This point will be discussed in Chapter 4 below.

And finally, the black taxis are accused of "raising money for terrorism." This kind of criticism is irrelevant to a report which is concerned only with transport characteristics. It might be noted, however, that nobody nowadays accuses franchised public transportation in U.S. cities of raising money for terrorism, or for any other purpose! Given the alleged interest of groups in Belfast to raise money for sectarian causes, it is significant that they chose to do so by providing shared taxi services, and further evidence for the general proposition advanced in this booklet that urban public transportation can make money, even in the West.

The Publicos of Puerto Rico

For the last 25 years the Commonwealth of Puerto Rico has had a dual system of public transportation: conventional buses operating along fixed routes and "Publicos" which are defined as "public automobile enterprises which includes any person other than taxi and tour enterprises, who as a public carrier, owns, controls, operates or manages in Puerto Rico any motor vehicle of a capacity not over 14 passengers . . ., over any public overland highway, regardless of whether or not such transportation is carried out between fixed or irregular terminals."

Most of the Publicos are owned by individuals and families and are driven by their owners. Fares are typically 50¢ (compared to 25¢ on the regular buses) and speeds are good. The vehicles are difficult to enter and exit, especially for elderly people, but ridership is encouraged by the "cleanliness and reliability" of the Publicos. The Publicos are licensed and supervised by the "Publico Service Commission" of the Commonwealth of Puerto Rico.

Following the decision of the federal government to phase out operating subsidies for public transportation, the Puerto Rico Department of Transportation is examining the possibilities of replacing some of its publicly-owned bus services (which recover from the fare box only 35% of the operating costs) by Publico services. A detailed study of Publicos in the city of Caguas (population 150,000), carried out in 1980, showed that about five-sixths of public transport trips were made by Publicos and one sixth by regular buses. It was found that, out of the 39 Publico routes studied in 1978, 29 were financially viable, 8 were not, and 2 had ceased operation. On average, daily costs per Publico vehicle in 1980, including interest and depreciation, were estimated to be in the range $60-65, while daily revenues averaged $74.

In comparison, bus operating costs in 1980 were estimated to be $154 per day, *exclusive* of depreciation. Revenues approximated $173, which meant that the bus system was financially viable only if the vehicles were obtained free or at very low cost. Caguas' public buses operate at a lower cost than those of San Juan because drivers are not unionized and maintenance costs and standards are lower, while fares are higher, than those prevailing in the capital city. Certainly the new, 45-seat buses provided to Puerto Rico for $140,000 each were not financially viable. It is noteworthy that Publico load factors, 76%-103%, were about double those of the buses which were 33%-50%.

The report concluded that the Publico car system was financially and economically viable and deserved to be supported fully. The bus system was found to be not viable if conventional buses were used, and the acquisition of 22-seat vehicles was recommended on the grounds that these vehicles would require no or small subsidies.

The report made a number of recommendations to improve the public transportation system. These included: constructing terminals and improving roads; strengthening the Public Service Commission; organizing an association of operators to provide service during non-rush hours, Sundays and holidays; and providing repair and maintenance shops. There was also a recommendation to increase the authorized capacity of the Publico from 14 to 17 passengers.

Other Systems

Limitations of space—and of the reader's patience—preclude detailed descriptions of:

- the rickshaws in China, in many cities often the only available method for transporting the elderly and handicapped;
- the pedicabs of Penang, which provide a local industry as well as a major transport mode;
- the motorized pedicabs of Karachi, which are economically accessible to many of those who cannot afford the regular taxi fare of US7¢ a mile;
- the *Kia-Kia* ("quick-quick") of Lagos, a service crucial to the life of that city;
- the *Fula-Fula* of Kinshasa, accused by visiting transportation experts as "interfering with traffic;"
- the *Por Puestos* (shared taxis) of Caracas, *Por Puesto* meaning "by the seat;"
- the shared intercity taxis that operate in Egypt, Israel, and between Malaysia and Singapore.

Sigurd Grava, who described many of the systems, summarized them as follows: "At first glance they all appear to be different, but this is primarily because of variations in hardware—from bicycle rickshaws to sleek European minibuses. The institutional structure and basic operations are quite similar: private individuals acquire the highest technology vehicle that they can afford, and respond to the mobility demands of their neighbors at a tariff that most of them can pay.... A few billion people cannot all be wrong, and there is really no need for us to painfully invent a new urban transportation mode when there are literally thousands of jitney systems in flourishing operation.''

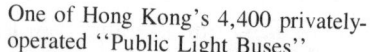

Minibuses in Kuala Lumpur traffic

One of Hong Kong's 4,400 privately-operated ''Public Light Buses''

3
Characteristics of Successful Public Transportation Systems

The systems described in Chapter 2, all of which are profitable, have the following characteristics:

- ownership is private;
- vehicles are small;
- operating units are small;
- route associations are part of many successful operations.

Ownership
That publicly-owned bus companies sustain losses is not entirely surprising as the systems taken over by public authorities tend to be the ones that cannot be run at a profit by private operators. However, the losses under public ownership tend to rise rapidly, at a rate that bears little relationship to increases in service levels. The losses appear to be due to (a) the higher cost levels (especially wages) that can be afforded by subsidized systems and (b) the inability of publicly-owned operators to resist pressures from politicians to hold down fares and expand unremunerative services. A few examples from developed and from developing countries can illustrate the point.

United States
When the Massachusetts Bay Transportation Authority (MBTA) was set up in 1964 as a public corporation, the system was operating at a deficit of about $15 million a year. By 1967, the managerial staff had doubled, the cost of office accommodation had soared, and the deficit had increased to $25 million. By 1980, the deficit had increased to $256 million and had become a burden that the local authorities were unable to meet. In the early 1970's the privately-owned bus service in Washington, D.C.—D.C. Transit—was in difficulty. Testimony before Congress indicated that the Washington area bus system could pay its own way from fare collections if

shifted from private to public ownership. It was duly taken over and ran a deficit of $8.5 million in 1973, its first calendar year. By 1974, the deficit had risen to around $40 million and by 1976 it reached $50 million, despite a doubling of the fare from 25¢ in 1973 to 50¢ in 1976. In fiscal 1981, the deficit on bus operations amounted to $101 million, up from $91 million a year earlier. The average fare meanwhile had risen to 69¢.

United Kingdom
In 1980, the U.K. Transport and Road Research Laboratory published a report on the economics of publicly- and privately-owned bus companies. A comparison of fares carried out in two areas showed that, for a wide range of journey lengths, the mean fare charged on rural and inter-urban runs by private operators was 25% lower than that charged on similar services provided by publicly-owned operators. Further economic analyses by the Laboratory indicated that the private operators' lower fares stemmed largely from lower unit costs, rather than from higher loads or other possible causes. The report concluded that at least some of these lower unit costs were due to the following factors:

- lower garage costs resulting from the use of low-cost premises;
- less expenditure on items associated specifically with large networks, e.g. bus stations, information offices, bus shelters and stop signs;
- lower staff costs resulting from greater flexibility. Part-time drivers were used and many full-time employees combined driving with administration or vehicle maintenance;
- lower staff costs resulting from lower wage rates and less advantageous working conditions. A 1978 survey indicated that the earnings of drivers in the private sector, although similar to the average for manual workers in all industries and services, were 10-15% lower than in the public sector;
- a greater proportion of one-man operations;
- lower loan repayments. Public sector companies tended to borrow more than those in the private sector and debt service costs were correspondingly higher;
- use of a greater proportion of smaller vehicles.

Thailand
In the early 1970's, Bangkok had 25 franchised bus companies, all of which provided service for a basic fare of about US4¢. The biggest company, the Nai Lert, managed by Khunying Loesak (a woman, later Minister of Transport), was consistently profitable. One of its distinguishing characteristics was that most of the buses, all single deckers, carried a crew of three, one

driver and two fare collectors. In 1976, following recommendations by European consultants, the government decided to amalgamate the 25 companies and to create the "Bangkok Metropolitan Transport Authority." The plan was carried through despite the protests of Khunying Loesak and many of the other operators. Shortly after the buses were taken over by the city, the fares were raised by 20% and yet the system started to operate at a deficit. By 1979, the BMTA was losing the equivalent of over US$25 million a year, while an estimated 7,000 privately-owned minibuses were running at a profit. The main reasons for the switch from profit to loss seem to have been improved wages to bus crews and reduced utilization of vehicles.

Australia

In 1975, 52% of the buses in New South Wales, 83% of those in Victoria and 46% of those in Queensland were private. In Queensland and Victoria the private operators were not allowed to raise fares to meet increased costs, but received government subsidies to enable them to stay in business. Thus, both privately-owned and publicly-owned bus operations in Australia were subsidized but, on average, the unit costs for private operators in Australian urban areas were found to be only between one-half and two-thirds of those of the publicly-owned operators providing similar services. Thus, in each city in which a comparison could be made, and in each year, the costs of the private operators were substantially lower than those of the public ones.

The reasons for the differences in costs were reported to have been due to differences in:

Crew Wage Rates. Basic wage rates for public operators' crews were about 11% higher than those for the private operators.

Labor Utilization and Flexibility. Some private operators, unlike the public services, employed part-time staff, though only a small proportion of their total employees. They also benefited from greater flexibility of staff. For example, many workers combined driving with other duties, thus minimizing the extra staff required to cover peak periods, sickness, etc. Almost all the staff of many private operators were able to drive buses and drove them when required. In particular, mechanics often carried out driving duties in peak periods, and drivers carried out much of the bus cleaning and routine maintenance work.

Maintenance and Administration. Private operators generally had smaller numbers of maintenance and administrative staff than public operators. The ratio of total employees to buses owned was typically 1.0-1.5 for private operators, but 2.0-2.5 for public operators. Although public operators often averaged a greater mileage per bus, the low proportion of non-driver staff employed by private operators made a substantial contribution to their lower costs. This factor alone has been estimated to result in total staff requirements for private operators to be 25% lower than for public ones. As labor costs were typically 70% of total bus company costs, this explains a 15-20% total cost saving for private operators.

Capital Facilities. In general, private operators tended to have older bus fleets than the public ones. Also, they tended to buy new buses more cheaply than the public operators and to buy used buses more frequently than the public operators. The different purchasing patterns reflected the difficulties that private operators, compared to public operators, had in finding funds for capital investment. Private operators also tended to have less elaborate and costly depot facilities than public operators, even allowing for their relative sizes. Many private operators had maintenance facilities in the open air rather than under cover and they provided very limited recreational facilities for staff—possibly a reflection of the little time their staff had for recreational activities.

It is noteworthy that, although private and public operators in Australia are exempt from sales tax on new buses, private operators are required to pay a 15% sales tax on all spare parts and tires, while public operators are exempt from this tax as well.

The typical operating costs of public and private bus operators in Australia are summarized in Table 3.1.

It may be concluded from experience worldwide that publicly-owned transport operators have higher costs than privately-owned ones, even when providing similar services, because they have less flexibility in making the best use of their resources and because they pay more to their employees. In transport, as in other fields (education, medical services and housing), the discipline of having to live within one's budget applies a constant downward pressure on costs, a pressure that is all too easily relieved by the availability of subsidies from public funds. Furthermore, the availability of subsidies makes it difficult for public sector companies to resist requests to provide—and even expand—unremunerative services.

Size of Vehicle

One of the established (but questionable) principles of public transportation operation is that large vehicles are more economical to operate than small ones. The reason given for this is that, with over two-thirds of bus operating costs being due to labor, it pays a bus company to have large vehicles, even if they are full for only a fraction of their working lives, so as to avoid the additional labor costs that would be required to meet peak demand with small vehicles. This reasoning, though perfectly logical, may be questioned for two reasons:

The first is that the capital cost *per seat* seems to increase with the size of the vehicle. For example, operators in San Juan, Puerto Rico, can expect to

TABLE 3.1
Typical Operating Costs—Public and Private Bus Operators in Australia

Cost Item	Public Operator (% of operating costs)	Private Operator (% of public operator costs)
Wage/salary and related costs:		
1. Driver wages	43.1[b]	30.2[b,c]
2. Traffic staff salaries	3.8	1.9[d]
3. Vehicle repairs/maintenance wages/salaries[a]	11.7	4.0[e]
4. Admin. and general salaries	3.9	2.5[f]
Total	62.5	38.6
5. Driver on-costs[g]	9.3	2.1[h]
6. Other staff on-costs[g]	3.7	1.0[i]
Total	13.0	3.1
Non-wage/salary costs:		
7. Direct operating costs fuel, tires, etc.	6.4	6.4[f]
8. Vehicle repairs/maintenance, materials, etc.[a]	3.7	2.7[f]
9. Depreciation	6.0	5.0[j]
10. Interest	3.2	3.5[k]
11. Insurances, licences and registration	3.5	4.5[j]
12. Miscellaneous general	1.7	1.0[l]
Total	24.5	23.1
Grand Total	100.0	64.8

Notes:
a. Includes workshop and spare parts costs.
b. Includes leave provisions.
c. Assumed 70% of public operator (see text).
d. Assumed 50% of public operator—in practice traffic staff also probably carry out other functions.
e. Assumed—from analysis of various private operators by comparison with public operators. In practice much of the maintenance carried out by drivers.
f. Assumed—based on inspection of various operators' accounts.
g. Includes payroll tax, and pension payments.
h. Assumed at 7% of private driver wages.
i. Assumed—represents 12% of private non-driver wages/salaries.
j. Assumed—see text.
k. Assumed—grants for new buses not generally available to private operators.
l. Assumed—allows for higher registration and license fees for private operators.

Source: I. Wallis, "Private Bus Operation in Urban Areas—Their Economics and Role." R. Travers Morgan Pty. Ltd., Australia, 1979.

pay $17,000 for a minibus seating 17, but $140,000 for a full-sized bus seating 50. Thus a full-sized bus can cost almost three times as much per unit of passenger capacity than a minibus. (Incidentally, the same pattern is evident when moving up to a rail car: a vehicle seating, say 150 passengers, can easily cost $1 million.) The main reason for this is that small vehicles can be mass produced and bought "off the shelf" while large ones tend to be made to special order and assembled as separate units.

But there is a second reason favoring the small bus which, while more subtle, may be more important. For a given route capacity, small buses provide more frequent service than large ones and, therefore, involve less waiting time per passenger. This factor might not matter to a franchised operator who has to bear the costs of his crew but not the waiting time of his customers; hence the preference of monopoly operators for big vehicles. However, where competition is allowed, those who provide public transportation have to respond to the needs of the passengers, most of whom dislike waiting for buses. To reduce waiting it is necessary to use small vehicles providing a frequent service. It is significant that when the private bus operators took over the municipal service in Buenos Aires in 1962 (page 12) one of their first actions was to replace the large municipal buses by smaller ones. More generally, whenever a private operator has the freedom to choose the size of his vehicle he generally chooses something less than a full-sized bus. The small bus has other advantages: as it holds fewer passengers, it is easier to fill with people starting at one point and wishing to travel to another, so it tends to stop less frequently than large buses; and, being more maneuverable, it can often make its way more quickly along congested streets.

Thus, while a bus operator might like to provide service using a small number of large buses, preferably crowded, with passengers having to wait a long time for their arrival, the public prefers the speed that can generally only be provided by small vehicles. These reasons may explain why, under conditions of competition, the smaller buses seem to have the edge over the larger ones.

Size of Operating Unit

Some businesses can only be operated by large firms. A manufacturing process requiring heavy capital investment cannot be operated as a backyard enterprise, as became evident during China's industrialization efforts. Other operations, such as a restaurant or beauty parlor, can be successfully provided by a single operator, a family firm, or a small partnership.

The organizational unit supplying public transportation ranges from the one-man bicycle rickshaw in East Asia to fleets containing thousands of buses in cities such as New York, Chicago, London, Bombay and Bangkok. Numbers of employees per bus also vary widely, from under 2 in Australia to 58 in the Office des Transports en Commun du Zaïre (OTCZ) of Kinshasa (as only about 50% of the OTCZ buses are on the road at any time, the staffing works out at 116 people per working bus). Attempts have been made to assess the effect of fleet size on the efficiency of public transportation systems but the results are not conclusive. A study comparing different sized firms in Britain reported that unit costs increase with fleet size, while the opposite effect was found in India. For the purpose of this report, it will be sufficient to note that there is no clear evidence that increases in the size of bus fleets result in lower costs or higher profitability.

On the other hand, there is clear evidence that large bus fleets incur financial losses under the same conditions that small operators—owner-drivers—turn to profits. Although operators the world over are reluctant to admit to making profits, the pressure to obtain permits to provide service and the prices at which permits in some cities change hands, or are hired out, are sure indications of profitability. In London, there is a well-documented case of a route that was given up by London Transport because it lost too much money, and was subsequently operated, without subsidy, by a private operator.

The reasons for the financial viability of the small transport firm, be it a mover, a taxi driver or a bus operator are well known and typical of other types of small business in the service sector. The owner will be willing to work longer and less regular hours than would a paid bus driver in a large fleet. He will clean his own vehicle (or enlist the help of family members) and is likely to do the routine servicing and maintenance himself. He will not have his own depot but will service his vehicle on the street or at a local garage. His record-keeping will be minimal; just sufficient to keep the tax inspector at bay. He will make a greater effort than a paid driver to collect fares from passengers and to ensure that the amounts collected do not get lost on the way. An extra driver can be employed if two shifts a day have to be run. Some facilities, such as a two-way radio service, can add to earnings without the owner relinquishing control of his vehicle.

There is also evidence that a high level of service over a wide area can be provided by small firms, as long as the organizational structure of the industry is appropriate. Taxis are a case in point. While some may be operated as one-man (or one-woman) firms and some in large fleets, there is no need for any formal coordination to achieve an acceptable level of service. Taxis find their way to where the business is most profitable and provide an example of *coordination through competition*. Obviously, a single operator cannot cover a whole route, but a route can be covered by a large number of individual operators organized, if necessary, as a route association.

In passenger transportation the basic operating unit is the vehicle and, as the taxi business proves, it is possible for the owner of even one vehicle to operate it successfully at a profit. Indeed, evidence from cities in Asia and Latin America suggests that it is possible for a group of people to own a small bus and to operate it at a profit. The owner-driver is in a particularly strong position to control the maintenance of his vehicle and the revenues obtained from customers. Hence there are real advantages to the operators of small transport units.

The Route Association
In order to make the maximum contribution in the provision of transportation, the individual unit does, however, have to work within an appropriate organizational framework. For example, a taxi looking for business has to be recognized by the public as being available for hire. If it is a vehicle intended to carry more than one person, its destination has to be clearly indicated. It is also important for the intending passenger to know the fare that is being charged, and the places at which vehicles can be readily found. Some of these features are provided by route associations which are to be found in many cities in Latin America, Africa and Asia.

The essence of the route association is that each vehicle remains under the control of its owner or owners, both as regard driving and maintenance. What is shared is the route, i.e. the members of the association ply a specified route, in conjunction with others, thus offering travelers a frequent service. Fares are generally fixed by the association, but not invariably: In Hong Kong and Istanbul, for example, higher fares are charged in peak periods when demand is higher and traffic congestion more acute (a similar system obtains for Washington, D.C. taxis, which are allowed to charge higher fares in peak periods than in off-peak ones). The revenues in some associations are retained by the individual members, and in others, pooled among the members.

The precise organization of a route association varies from city to city. Any group operating a route has an interest in limiting its numbers and also in ensuring that its members work harmoniously with one another. This means that conditions must be imposed on entry (possibly an entrance fee) and that rules are laid down to prevent members from "stealing" traffic from following vehicles by traveling behind their schedules. However, in many cities (Buenos Aires, Manila, Calcutta, Hong Kong) route associations compete with one another so that no group has a monopoly over an entire route. There are also reports of infighting between competing groups of operators. However, the route associations definitely work, serving both the public and their members.

Disadvantages of Informal Public Transportation
Private enterprise public transportation has disadvantages as well as advantages. Sigurd Grava has listed them as follows:

Service is provided only if it is profitable. This disadvantage, which applies to any commodity provided by private enterprise, certainly holds. In general, only a monopoly or franchised operation can subsidize unprofitable routes out of the earnings of profitable ones. However, *cross-subsidization* of this kind is an inefficient way to help people who cannot afford to pay the full costs of public transportation, as discussed in Chapter 4.

Low-density or poor neighborhoods remain unserviced. Although this criticism is often made, there are many places in which it is not valid. For example, in Nairobi, and in many Latin American cities, it is only the informal sector that serves the poor neighborhoods.

The high competitiveness of the activity can keep the income of drivers at the bottom level. This again, is true, but that is part of the price of keeping fares down. Furthermore, many of the drivers who work at relatively low wages providing public transportation earn more than they could in other occupations. And many earn substantial wages—enough to enable them to buy their vehicles.

There are opportunities for illegal operations, even for gangsterism. It is true that in some cities the methods used by route associations to protect their "territory" can be criminal, unlawful, perhaps even homicidal. But the institution of "protection" is not confined to unregulated transport systems. It behooves society at large to protect the public interest through its law enforcement agencies.

The scramble for fares necessitates an undisciplined attitude and behavior toward traffic regulations. This seems to be a fair criticism, but one that applies to the taxi business in many cities. And private motorists are often no better. Here, too, a strict enforcement of traffic rules can cope with anti-social behavior.

Public agencies tend to ignore informal transportation, and even to eliminate it, since it does not present a "proper civic image." This is very true, particularly in developing countries where national leaders bent on projecting a prestigious image are often embarrassed by small-scale free enterprise, one of the best things they have going. However, this is hardly a valid criticism.

Maintenance of equipment can be deficient, at a cost to safety. This can be a valid criticism, though it is fair to point out that operators of any transport system have strong incentives to avoid accidents. Local government inspection systems and regulations can help cope with this problem.

The regularity and reliability of service can be affected by the whims of owners and drivers. This again is a valid criticism, which, however, loses much of its strength in places where there are large numbers of operators.

These, then, are some of the reported characteristics of free enterprise urban public transportation outside the U.S. Let the readers decide whether such systems could be used to advantage in their own communities.

Caracas' "Por Puestos" (by the seat) jitneys cruise the main arteries

A Chiang Mai (Thailand) shared taxi operating in excess of capacity

4
Application in the U.S.: Possibilities and Problems

Requirements of U.S. Urban Transportation Users
Before considering the possibilities of "informal" public transportation services in the U.S., it is necessary to describe some of the characteristics of travel in U.S. cities and to ask why more than 90% of motorized trips are made by private automobile rather than by public transportation. Commentators frequently attribute the flight from conventional transit to some irrational "love affair with the automobile" and suggest that, if only Americans behaved sensibly, they would switch from private to public transport, at least for the journey to work.

This view is superficial and misleading. People travel to increase the opportunities available to them, i.e., opportunities to live in pleasant surroundings, to work for desirable employers, to shop in desirable places, to be entertained, to meet friends, to be educated. As people get richer, they do not, as a rule, use their wealth to re-arrange their activities so as to reduce travel; on the contrary, in the U.S., as in other societies, travel tends to increase with income. This may be illustrated by Figure 4.1, which shows how, in 1977, average daily travel distance per household in Baltimore increased as income increased. The increase in total distance traveled was due both to increases in average trip lengths and to increases in the numbers of trips per household.

But how can people increase the distances they travel? One way would be to spend more of their time in travel. But, as people grow richer, their time becomes more valuable and they tend to spend less, rather than more, time on travel. People constrained by a shortage of time—as most of us are—can only increase their travel by traveling faster. And, indeed, the Baltimore data (Figure 4.2) show that travel speeds there increased with income.

This was due, of course, to the higher automobile ownership associated with increasing income; and Figure 1 shows clearly that the increased travel per household was, on average, due to increased travel by automobile, not by bus.

39

It is to be expected, then, that as incomes rise in the future—as they are most likely to do—people will tend to seek faster modes of travel to enable them to make the most of the spatial opportunities available to them. Speed is, of course, recognized to be the main factor in the choice of travel modes not only in the U.S., but all over the world. It follows, therefore, that the surest way to enable public transport to compete with the private car is to raise its door-to-door speed.

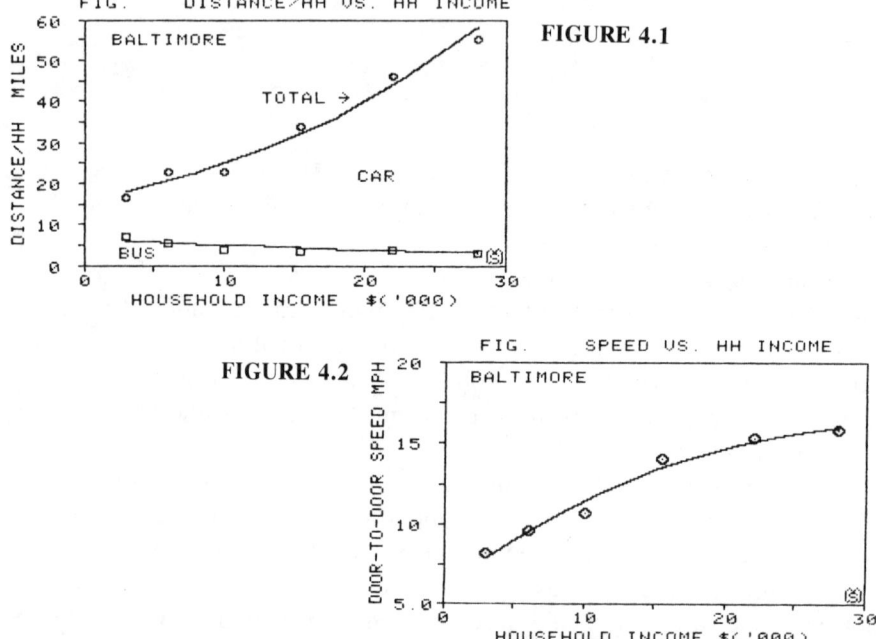

FIGURE 4.1

FIGURE 4.2

This may be illustrated by the case of New York, London, and other cities having mass transit systems on their own rights-of-way, which can travel relatively quickly irrespective of congestion on the streets. In such cities mass transportation patronage has held up through the years despite the atrocious discomfort of peak-hour travel. Many people will put up with uncomfortable travel, if it gives them the chance of staying in bed a few minutes longer or living in congenial surroundings.

A second key characteristic of American urban dwellers is their desire to live at low density. Some planners disapprove of low-density living and refer to it disparagingly as "sprawl." Despite a significant movement of the childless and the unmarried to city centers, the mainstream of American population movement is still from city centers to suburbs, and from high-density areas (in the Northeast) to low-density ones (in the South and West). But suburban living cannot be efficiently served by fixed-route bus or rail lines: fast door-to-door service in low-density neighborhoods can only be provided by a transport mode flexible enough to arrive quickly close to people's homes in response to their needs.

Given, then, the desire of city dwellers for transportation that is both *fast* and *flexible*, how would they choose to travel? Private transportation has obvious advantages, but it also has disadvantages: it is expensive if it cannot be shared, and it is not available to some classes of travelers such as the very young, the very old, the infirm and those not licensed to drive. What are the alternatives? Bicycles can be used for some trips, and legs for others, but many journeys require motorized public transportation. Taxis are estimated to account for about 40% of all the trips provided by public transportation in the U.S., but they are expensive if used in the dominant single occupancy mode. How can speedy and flexible public transport be provided economically? One approach is to provide speedy public transport by dedicating to it a reserved right-of-way. This is the prime advantage of the railway and of the "busway." As railway trains cannot provide service away from their track, they cannot satisfy the requirements of both speed and flexibility except in very special situations, e.g., journeys that start and finish in the vicinity of the same railway line. Reserved busways—or bus lanes on highways—are better suited to accommodate flexible public transport services, as they can provide uninterrupted runs over long distances by vehicles that can pick up and set down passengers close to the origins and destinations of their journeys. Such busways, or buslanes, can accommodate full-sized buses, minibuses, vanpools and even carpools.

The expense of private transportation and that of rapid transit systems on their own rights-of-way have been mentioned. Experience has shown, however, that Americans are not deterred by expensive transportation services; on the contrary, many seem to be put off by low-cost services, such as those provided by the conventional bus, believing that the low cost must be an indication of poor quality. But high-quality bus services can be successful. An express bus operation with premium fares has been operating in New York City since 1968; its success has spawned more than 30 additional public and private express routes.

Let us then, in our pursuit of excellence, consider what would be likely to be the most desirable form of public transportation for low-density American cities, irrespective of cost. The answer might well be shared taxis or minibuses, collecting people from a group of destinations close to one another, and traveling nonstop to another group of destinations. Indeed, unless travelers can park at their destinations, a shared taxi or minibus might even provide faster service than a private car. For example, travelers from the bedroom community of Reston travel by a minibus "subscription service" to government offices in the center of Washington in 50 minutes; travel by regular bus would take them 60 minutes and by private car 45 minutes—possibly more—depending on the time spent in parking. Thus, while the minibus may not always be quite as fast as the private car, it is considerably faster than conventional transit and it is also cheaper. An unsubsidized daily round trip in the case of Reston costs a rider $61 a month compared to $90 by the heavily subsidized conventional bus, and over $200 by private car if all costs (including parking) are taken into account.

Existing Free-Enterprise Urban Public Transportation Services in the U.S.A.

But, if small, informal, self-financing systems can really work, why are they not provided by free enterprise? The answer is simple but not satisfying. Such services were provided in the first quarter of the century, but many were outlawed in the 1920s and are generally still illegal in U.S. cities. There is evidence, however, that a new trend is starting and some free enterprise unsubsidized public transportation services, in addition to exclusive-use taxicabs, can be identified in the U.S. today.

Pedicabs

Let's start with pedal power. Unless you've been to Honolulu recently you probably didn't know that over a hundred pedicabs are doing a thriving business in the capital of the 50th state, mainly along Waikiki beach. The three-wheeled, hooded vehicles propelled by able-bodied pedal pushers who charge up to $5 for a 15 minute trip are modeled after the pedicabs of Southeast Asia. Hawaii's gentle climate and relaxed lifestyle favor this kind of transportation which would hardly be appropriate to, say, Boston or New York. During the rainy season the resourceful drivers protect their passengers with plastic covers and often beat out taxis in picking up rides because of their sheer numbers. The largest of the free-wheeling firms, Open Air Pedicab Company, was founded by two New Yorkers who needed a change of pace.

Shared Taxis

Shared taxi services are formally licensed in only a tiny fraction of the 3,360 incorporated U.S. communities with a population of over 5,000 which are known to be served by taxicabs. Shared services are run in Albuquerque (N.Mex.), Chapel Hill (N.C.), Daytona Beach (Fla.), Denver (Col.), Indianapolis (Ind.), Little Rock (Ark.), Los Angeles (Ca.), Miami (Fla.), Meriden (Conn.), Montgomery (Ala.), Minneapolis (Minn.), Norfolk (Va.), Phoenix (Ar.), Pittsburgh (Pa.), Portland (Ore.), Red Bank (N.J.), Seattle (Wa.), Washington (D.C.) and Westport (Conn.). Little Rock has had a successful shared taxi system for decades. In Washington, D.C., taxis occupied by one or more passengers often stop to pick up other passengers going in the same direction. The licensing authority for the Washington, D.C., area has specified permissible fares for shared taxis, but these are not widely known to travelers and, in general, each occupant of a shared cab pays the full, single-occupancy, rate.

Illegal shared services are provided in New York and many other cities, large and small. *The New York Times* reported that "in Chicago, scores of (illegal jitneys) can be seen daily. They travel along King Street, stopping at street corners or in mid-block to pick up housewives with shopping bags, youths, and other people. For a quarter, they ride a few blocks through the black South Side." In small holiday resorts, illegal shared rides are the only transport mode available to enable low-income hotel workers to get to work.

All the above services are financially viable in the sense that the full costs are paid by the riders, with no subsidy. But there are also many shared taxi systems in which the taxis are employed by public agencies on a contract basis as an alternative requiring less subsidy than conventional transit on the less-traveled routes.

Shared taxi services have enormous potential to benefit both the taxi industry and taxi users, but it is difficult to envisage much progress in this direction without the development of contractual arrangements that would benefit both sides. A fare system for shared-taxi riding should have the following characteristics:

- Fares should be easily calculated, preferably in advance, and be readily understood by passengers, drivers, companies and regulators,
- Shared-ride fares should offer reductions for passengers as well as increased revenues for companies and for drivers,
- The option for exclusive riding—at exclusive ride fares—should be available to passengers,
- Cross-subsidizing some trips from revenues received from others should be minimized.

It is possible that a taxi meter will be devised that can offer a fare structure that will meet these requirements. However, it has been convincingly argued that a meter is unlikely to fit the bill, as it cannot properly account for the route deviations that are inevitably associated with shared riding. Some of the schemes put forward do not use meters but rather zone systems, as the basis for fares. At least three schemes are available:

- The Meriden flat-fare scheme for shared-taxi rides;
- The Fine Grid scheme, proposed by the Urban Institute;
- The Ride Shared Vehicle Paratransit (RSVP) system developed at Carnegie-Mellon University.

The Meriden flat fare system. The management of the Meriden Yellow Cab Company attaches great importance to shared-taxi riding, in which it sees enormous potential for the future. While using the standard taxi meter for exclusive rides, it experimented with a zone system for shared riding. However, the zone system was found to be complicated and was replaced by a flat fare of $1.70 ($1.20 plus 50¢ fuel surcharge) for journeys within an area of 22 square miles. Customers requiring shared-taxi rides—for example for the journey to work—telephone the company the day before and place their orders for both outward and homeward journeys. The dispatchers at the taxi company make up taxi-loads of people, all of whom pay the flat fare of $1.70. This scheme has increased early morning and evening ridership appreciably. The customer still has the option of requiring an exclusive taxi, in which case he is billed on the meter. Many of the Meriden Yellow Cab Company drivers provide shared ride services in the morning and evenings, and revert to exclusive use at other times.

Urban Institute "grid" fare structure. The Urban Institute, a think tank in Washington, D.C., which has done considerable work on urban transport problems, proposes the adoption of a zone system; the zones are delineated by a fine grid dividing the urban area into roughly half-mile squares. Each passenger would originate in one sub-area and terminate either in that same sub-area or in another. The fare would be based on the number of contiguous sub-areas which lie between the passengers' trip origin and trip destination. The driver and passenger would simply agree upon the smallest number of contiguous steps required for a taxi to travel directly from origin to destination and which would provide the basis of the fare. The rate structure could be similar to that currently used for exclusive ride services: a fixed charge for the first step (corresponding to the current "flag drop"), and a small charge for each additional step. Different rates could be applied for exclusive rides and shared rides. In areas of significant traffic congestion, it would be possible to charge higher rates for travel during rush hours, as is already done in Washington, D.C.

A scheme similar to that proposed by the Urban Institute was, in fact, used for many years by the Black and White Checker Cab Company in Little Rock, Ark. Subsequently, it was introduced in Montgomery, Ala., and in Minneapolis, where it seems to be working to the satisfaction of the transit commission and taxicab companies. The rates are $1.55 for the first sub-area and 60¢ for each additional one.

The Ride Shared Vehicle Paratransit (RSVP) system. The People's Cab Company of Pittsburgh, owned by the Center for Entrepreneurial Development, a nonprofit corporation affiliated with Carnegie-Mellon University, introduced the RSVP system to deal with shared rides. The RSVP can be regarded as the ultimate in zone systems, in that fares are calculated by computer on a point to point basis on the strength of geographic data stored in it. Taxi drivers radio the origins and destinations of proposed trips to the computer and receive in response the appropriate fare. Customers agreeing to that fare are not charged extra for route deviations which inevitably occur when rides are shared—each traveler pays for travel only from the trip origin to destination. For shared riding, fares are discounted at an agreed rate, which in the summer of 1981 was 10%.

The International Taxicab Association (ITA), representing operators in both the U.S. and Canada, encourages the adoption of shared ride systems in all localities where they are not already present. An ITA policy statement and representative shared ride ordinances are reproduced in the Annex.

Contract Services

In principle, there is nothing to stop any public agency, such as a transit commission, from inviting private firms to bid for the right to provide certain services. If the services are known to be unprofitable, the invitation would be in the form of "how much do you want to be paid in order to guarantee a service at agreed times and frequencies?" This kind of operation has been organized in a particularly effective manner in Knoxville, Tenn., where a Transportation Broker Office was set up for the purpose of seeking out transportation suppliers and inducing them to provide services specified by major employers, hospitals, and social service agencies in the Knoxville area.

Some transportation authorities have started to contract with private operators to replace services operated by the public agencies themselves. For example, the Tidewater Transportation District Commission (TTDC), which is responsible for public transportation in the Norfolk area, recently substituted privately-contracted taxis for poorly supported bus services. While the ridership associated with these changes increased in some cases and declined in others, costs and deficits invariably fell. In low-density residential areas and in the evenings where bus service has proved to be inappropriate and uneconomical, local taxicab companies are contracted to provide door-to-door "demand-responsive" service in its place. Contractors are selected on the basis of qualifications and bid cost per vehicle hour. The TTDC also owns vans and buses and leases them to individual companies for commuting. In 1981, approximately 100 vans (minibuses) and 12 buses were leased. The revenues from the leases covered 100% of capital, maintenance and insurance costs and a portion of administrative costs. The TTDC also leases vehicles to private operators such as a limousine company which provides shuttle service to and from a naval installation, an athletic association for transporting its members to events, and a health agency for transporting clients. Terms of the leases vary, but usually include the TTDC's

Tidewater Regional Transit (Norfolk, Va.) operates vanpools to reduce deficits

When the snow flies and the mercury falls, the Commute-A-Van program has extra appeal for 3M Company employees in Minnesota

provision of equipment and maintenance, and the lessee's provision of drivers, insurance and fuel. The TTDC's price includes capital recovery, maintenance, administration and profit margin of about 20%.

Jeff Becker, Service Development Manager of the TTDC, comments:

> We are continually trying to expand our line of services in order to provide as wide a range of alternative services to meet the public transportation needs of Tidewater citizens. By working with the private sector, we hope to stimulate additional services at low or no cost to the public. TTDC believes that a wide range of competitive and complementary, privately and publicly provided transportation services will ensure adequate and economical transportation for its constituents.

Other cities in which taxis are substituting for buses include Arabi (La.), Westport and Chapel Hill. In California, over 50 publicly-supported community transit services, some for the general public, some restricted to the elderly and handicapped, are operated by taxi firms under contract to public agencies.

Subscription Services
Subscription services involve a group of passengers contracting (subscribing) for the supply of a bus or minibus on a regular basis for journeys to and from work. The driver is either supplied by the vehicle contractor or provided by the travelers. One of the largest and oldest subscription bus operations is COM-BUS, which was established in 1967 in California to enable employees of the McDonnell-Douglas Corporation to reach a plant 50 miles away from their homes. As in some other cases, the services were started by a group of travelers after the local transit agency refused to provide service with its own vehicles. Similar services exist all over the U.S. They are characterized by comfort (e.g. seats for all), reliability, and higher door-to-door speeds than can be provided by regular transit. These services generally operate without subsidy, except for free parking facilities granted by employers. The fare charged on the Reston subscription service referred to earlier approximates 5¢ a mile, which covers all costs including a profit to the bus operator.

The disadvantage of subscription services is their schedule inflexibility, though even this can be overcome if the service is large enough to support a group of vehicles running at different times. The time advantage over conventional transit arises from not having to stop over the long-haul segment of the journey. This makes subscription services particularly popular for long-distance commuting.

Van Pools

Van pools, like subscription services, involve a group of 8-12 employees contracting to travel to and from work in a minibus on a regular basis. They differ from subscription services in that the vehicles generally belong to, or are leased by, employers and in that drivers are members of the van pooling group and drive at no charge. Typically, the drivers are remunerated by being allowed to travel free and to have the use of the minibuses for evenings and weekends either free or at nominal rates.

The first van pool system to achieve national fame was the one introduced in 1973 by the 3M Company in St. Paul (Minn.). The 3M van pool program was an attempt to prove that the total number of automobiles used for the work trip could be significantly reduced, thereby alleviating congestion and reducing the demand for parking. Environmental considerations such as energy savings and air pollution were also concerns, though not major objectives of the program. At first, six van pools, each consisting of a "pool coordinator" and a minimum of eight paying passengers, at least one of whom was a back-up driver, were formed. The passengers paid on a monthly basis for a reserved seat. In selling the service, emphasis was placed on its exclusive nature and on its comfort and door-to-door service. The pool coordinator was compensated with a free ride, personal use of the vehicle, and all passenger fares over the minimum of eight. The back-up driver was paid by the coordinator when he drove, and also was allowed occasional personal use of the vehicle. Within a short period it was evident that the van pool concept was very successful and popular with the participants. Extreme interest was generated among other 3M employees as well as in other industries. Long waiting lists of employees and self-formed groups waiting for additional vehicles began to appear. In July 1973, the 3M management decided to expand the program, which now includes 150 van pools. The 3M company did not desire to profit from the operation of the program nor did it wish to have the program regarded as a subsidy to those participating. The monthly fare structure was therefore determined on the basis that all costs, including the purchase cost of the vehicle depreciated over a four year period, would be covered. A typical cost schedule for a van pool is shown in Table 4.1.

Van pooling expanded rapidly in the 1970s. In 1976, the National Association of Van Pool Operators (NAVPO) was founded to represent the large corporate van pool sponsors. The NAVPO membership has doubled every year since its foundation in 1976, and its executive director predicts that the number of employer-sponsored van pools could jump from the 1981 figure of about 12,000 to as many as 100,000 by 1985 and to 500,000 by 1990. It is noteworthy that van pooling in the U.S. is growing at a much faster rate than car pooling, which has only grown by a modest 10% since 1970. In ad-

TABLE 4.1
Commute-A-Van Calculations
(for 1981)

A. FIXED COSTS

Cost of Vehicle $11,000.00
Immediate Depreciation 200.00
Cost for Depreciation Purposes 10,800.00

Monthly charges
1. Depreciation over 60 months 180.00
2. Insurance 27.00
3. One-Time Fixed Costs—First Year
   Sales Tax $440
   Tires 200
   License 43
4. One-Time Fixed Costs—2nd-5th Years
   License (Average) 120
5. Total One-Time Fixed Costs—60 Months 13.38
6. Total Monthly Cost for 60 Months 220.38
7. Estimated Value of Vehicle after
   60 Months is $1,800, or by month 30.00
8. Monthly Fixed Cost to be Received by
   User Income (6 minus 7) is $2284.56/year or 190.38

7. Yearly Fixed Cost Used for Fare
   Calculation Purposes $2,286.00

TOTAL MONTHLY COST PER VEHICLE 190.50

B. OPERATING COSTS   Cost per mile
1. Gasoline at $1.39 (9 mpg) .... $.155
2. Oil Change, Filter & Lube
   at 5,000 mile intervals ($22.00 each) .... .005
3. Maintenance .... .055
4. Tires (Cost for Life of Vehicle) .... .015
5. Total Operating Costs .... .230

dition to the corporate van pools represented in the NAVPO, there is also significant growth among independent owner-operated van pools. For example, the New Jersey DOT's Office of Ride-sharing estimates that for every one of the 1,500 employer-sponsored van pools operating in New Jersey there are as many as four independent van pools on the road.

The success of van pools is undoubtedly due to their ability to offer users a combination of speed, comfort and economy. The speed is a reflection of the door-to-door service. The comfort is related to the quality of the vehicles used. These are often equipped with carpets, air-conditioning, bucket seats and tape recorders with individual earphones (the latter probably particularly valuable in giving riders the option of not having to converse with their neighbors). Some van pools offer additional luxuries such as newspapers, beer and card games. Commuters who normally would drive to work say they can save between $1 and $3 a day in travel expenses by van pooling. It reduces wear and tear on autos and lowers the expenses of parking and fuel. On average, each van pool reduces by eight the number of cars in rush hour traffic and it gets about 150 passenger miles to the gallon. Some van poolers report lower insurance rates on their own cars because they ride van pools to work.

Companies say van pools boost employee morale, reduce absenteeism, and broaden the territory from which they can attract workers. They also help solve the costly problem of providing individual parking spaces for employees. The Tennessee Valley Authority, which operates 375 vans, included only limited parking facilities when it built its new Knoxville headquarters in 1976. The estimated saving was $5 million. Because van pooling employees arrive and leave on a precise schedule, efficiency is improved and overtime kept to a minimum. The essential business gets done during core hours.

Congressional Budget Office figures published by the Highway Users Federation put the average cost per passenger mile for a 10-mile, one-way, commuting trip in a large metropolitan area at 5.7¢ for a 10 member van pool, compared to 23.1¢ for a bus and 29.7¢-36.1¢ for rail transit. A typical van pool commuting from New Jersey to the Rockefeller Center costs each member $45 per month, or 4.2¢ per passenger mile, which includes more than $100 per month for a parking space in the Rockefeller Center. The alternative, by bus or subway, would cost passengers at least $80 per month, despite substantial taxpayer subsidies of the public systems, and take more time. The Department of Transportation notes that in 1979 membership in a van pool saved each commuter who previously drove to work in his own car an average $883 a year.

New Jersey is by no means unique in the number of its van pools. Houston, which claims to be the "van pool capital of the nation" has about 1,500 van pools, and the mode is also growing rapidly in California and Seattle. Some of the vehicles used for van pooling are owned by transit agencies (as in Seattle) or by private organizations set up specifically to promote van pooling (Commuter-Computer in Los Angeles, RIDES in San Francisco and Vango in Baltimore). And many vehicles are provided—at a profit—by private companies like Hertz and the Chrysler Corporation. Hertz even provides a corporate "turnkey" program that furnishes the required vans, maintenance, forms, insurance and a hotline to a company trouble shooter in charge of the account. Over 500 vans in 24 companies are already a part of the arrangement.

Jitneys

The use of five- or six-seat passenger vehicles for public transport was known in western American cities by 1910. Typically, model T Fords would cruise along the route of a downtown trolley line picking up passengers and delivering them as close to their destination as the driver deemed possible without a major diversion of the other passengers. These vehicles were called "jitneys," because the charge was a jitney (5¢) a ride. The term is said to orginate from the French *jeton* or token.

The jitney movement spread rapidly. By 1915 their number was estimated to have reached 62,000 and in the same year a trade magazine, "The Jitney Bus," was founded. Some of the operators were full-timers while others were men who simply displayed on their vehicles their places of work when they left home and picked up anyone willing to pay for a ride along the way. Some men drove as jitney operators for an hour or two before or after work. The 1914 recession attracted many men into the jitney business, particularly those who had bought automobiles but found themselves without the means to pay for them.

The jitneys had an immediate effect on the revenues of the franchised services which promptly lobbied to regulate the innovation out of existence. They were largely successful, so that, by 1919, most of the jitney services were driven out of business by local ordinances, such as those requiring the operators to obtain franchises or to post viability bonds. Other regulations, such as those requiring jitney operators to offer their services for a minimum number of hours each day or to specify in advance their precise routes and time schedules, eliminated the jitneys' competitive advantages in providing flexible, specialized service, particularly in the peak periods.

The attitude of the franchised operators can be illustrated by a consultant's report on the St. Louis "Service Cars," an association of jitney operators that was formed in the 1920's and continued until 1965. In 1957 W. C. Gilman reported that, on the routes on which they competed, the Service Cars accounted for 70% of all public trips and about 50% of peak-hour trips. He also reported that they charged the same fare as the franchised streetcars, guaranteed seats to all who could get on them, ran more frequently than the streetcars, and, because of fewer intermediate stops and the ability to dodge traffic, usually made better time than the streetcars, despite the latter's right-of-way over portions of the routes. However, Mr. Gilman recommended against continuation of the Service Cars, stating:

> Although the Service Cars offer a more frequent service than could be given a similar passenger volume by either streetcars or buses, this is not sufficient justification for their parasitical activity. Operation of this type of transit service has a capacity of only

8 persons as compared to the 50 or more seats in a transit vehicle. Since individually-operated vehicles cannot be expected to exchange transfers, general coverage of the city by Service Cars, instead of transit, would require about half of the riders to pay two fares. Competitive services of this character should not be permitted. They can survive only in areas where there is heavy transit riding, and these are the areas in which an area-wide transit system needs all of the business to average out the thin areas in which noncompensatory service is being operated.

The criticisms that small-capacity vehicles are "extremely wasteful of street space" and that the operators of large transit vehicles have to be protected to "average out the thin areas" can be heard even today and are as invalid today as they were when Mr. Gilman uttered them. The low priority given to service frequency by a transport expert seems strange, and the use of the term "parasitical" to describe a service provided in the market by willing sellers to willing buyers reflects the heat of the battle which was won by the franchised operators, not by providing better service than the jitneys, but by restrictive legislation. It should, however, be noted that jitneys were associated with an increase in accidents in virtually every city and that minor accidents involving jitneys competing for passengers at the curbs were common. Jitneys were also reportedly used for abduction, robbery, and rape both by drivers and by passengers who commandeered vehicles. These problems inevitably helped the political opponents of the jitneys to bring them down.

The victory of the buses and streetcars was almost complete—some jitney services operate to this day—but only temporary. By the 1970's the streetcar and many bus lines were in turn defeated by the private automobile and the suburbanization that it brought about. Tracks were torn up and rights-of-way dismantled to provide more street space for the private car.

In 1976, George Hilton commented:

> Had the jitneys been allowed to survive they probably would have driven the electric streetcars out of existence except on the most heavily-traveled routes by the mid-1920s. The urban transportation system in our major cities would consist mainly of competitive owner-operated vehicles. These would range from private automobiles registered as common carriers through specialized vehicles like Volkswagen microbuses and American van vehicles run by full-time operators to a smaller number of 40 to 50 passenger diesel buses like those that currently operate in the indus-

try. Jitneys would operate without restriction as to route, schedule, or fare. They could accordingly operate faster because of free choice of route and, being in the main smaller, they would be able to operate longer distances without stopping. Judging from the tolerated jitney service on the Martin Luther King Drive in Chicago, they could apparently provide a higher standard of service than such entities as the Chicago Transit Authority for about 60% of the cost and still yield a profit.

The road back may indeed have started. A jitney service—provided by 15-passenger minibuses labeled "JITNEY" operated by the Yellow Cab Company in Indianapolis—went into service in May 1981. The owner of the company, Richard Hunt, had to spend 18 months and $30,000 in legal fees to obtain the permit to run the service which receives no subsidy. The main opposition was put up by the local transit authority which was receiving massive capital and operating subsidies. On the other hand, San Diego, which favors competition and has deregulated entry into the transport field, now sports a fleet of 25 jitneys. Only time will tell if jitney services will be reincarnated over here as a viable, self-financing public transportation mode.

Route Associations
The existence of route associations in Buenos Aires, Calcutta and Manila was noted in Chapter 2. Such associations also exist in the U.S., the biggest and best developed concentration probably being in New Jersey.

Bus operation has a long tradition in New Jersey; some of the companies are linked to railways and streetcars that operated at the turn of the century. The early part of the century saw the development of many jitney services, from which some of the services operating today can be traced.

Around 40% of New Jersey's buses, approximately 1,400 of 3,000, which provide services within cities and between them, are still privately run. Most of the existing companies are small, with many buses driven by their owners. In order to provide services over a route, some of the operators are grouped in associations of different kinds. The only things they have in common are that schedules are coordinated and that each member of every association must operate profitably and be financially independent. They manage to stay solvent for reasons of private initiative at work from Australia to Zaïre even though their fares are at least 10% lower than the state-owned New Jersey Transit buses.

Some of the associations, such as Lafayette Greenville, Montgomery West Side, Central Avenue, and Bergen Avenue, share not only the routes, but also the revenues. This discourages the members from competing for the most profitable routes. There are, however, associations of operators who share routes without pooling the receipts. In the case of the Springfield Avenue Bus Association each operator retains the revenues collected on his buses. The associations operate on a coordinated schedule. Many of the operators provide commuter service to New York, with the inter-state revenues occasionally making up for losses incurred on intra-state runs. The private buses can be seen streaming into the Port Authority bus terminal along the exclusive busway provided by the Authority for use during the morning rush-hour period.

Buses are regulated in New Jersey. To be allowed to provide services, an operator has to show that he has safe equipment and competent drivers. In order to join an association, a newcomer would have to bargain with it, either buying the share of an existing member or meeting other conditions set by the association. If a company or association wishes to serve a completely new route, permission has to be obtained from the licensing authority which, before granting permission, may take into account objections from other operators. The heavily-subsidized New Jersey Transit, which is currently running $50 million a year in the red, often objects to competition from non-subsidized independents who wish to run at their own risk and expense.

Obstacles to the Growth of Free Enterprise Public Transportation

Although free enterprise public transportation has proved itself able—both in the U.S. and overseas—to provide high-quality services at low cost and without subsidy, most large cities cling to the slower, more costly, franchised services provided by large fleets of large vehicles operating along fixed routes. Why?

The answer seems to stem from the economics of the franchising system under which operators of conventional public transportation provide a range of services, some low-cost and some high-cost, in the areas designated by their franchise. Although the costs of providing these services vary widely, fares tend to be uniform over the system so there are large variations in the profitability of its different elements. The essence of the franchise system is "cross-subsidization," i.e., the more-profitable elements are supposed to support the less-profitable. Operators therefore resist competition on the ground that competitors would "cream-off" the more-profitable services and leave the franchised operators with the obligation to provide those that show the biggest losses. This consideration raises questions of two kinds:

- Would conventional transit systems be able to compete with "informal" ones?
- What would happen to travelers on "weak" public transportation routes in the absence of a franchised operator required to provide service?

Effect of Competition on Existing Transportation Services

We have seen that, both in the U.S. and overseas, the main opposition to unregulated, free-enterprise public transportation has come from the established franchised services. Operators of such services have traditionally behaved as if competition would make their tasks more difficult. This fear might be justified if the franchised services had to continue the provision of unprofitable operations, while losing the low-cost, profitable ones to competitors free to take the "cream" of the traffic available. We contend that:

- If franchised services were to lose their protection from competition, they should also be relieved of the obligation to provide high-cost, loss-incurring services for which other subsidy arrangements should be made.
- If relieved of such obligations, they might be better off in the end under competitive conditions than as monopoly franchises.
- The fact that they could become worse off under competition is not, in itself, a sufficient reason to restrain the competition and its built-in impetus for cost-efficiency.

Until October 1980, the British National Bus Company (NBS) was given substantial protection against competition on its main inter-urban routes and, in exchange, had to provide a service to low-density rural areas. Legislation passed in 1980 abolished both the protection and the obligations, and the NBC was left to do its best in a competitive market. NBC officials were concerned about the people in rural areas who, it was believed, would lose their public transport (though legislation was also passed to enable local needs to be met by local "informal" services) but had no fears with regard to their ability to maintain service on main routes. Competition on these routes did in fact appear and resulted in dramatic fare reductions—50% in some cases—but the company appears to have had no difficulty in maintaining its share of profitable routes. Its total volume on long distance routes increased from 8-9 million trips a year to 12 million, with massive increases in service on certain routes, notably those from London to the Midlands and the Northwest. For example, a half-hourly service was provided on the 100-mile London-Birmingham route, whereas before de-regulation there were journeys only every 2-1/2 hours.

The U.S. franchised operators are often in a similar situation. They operate under the major handicap of having to provide a mix of service, high-cost and low-cost, without the possibility of charging higher fares for the services that cost them more to provide.

One of the most severe burdens that has to be carried by the franchised operators is the requirement to meet the morning and evening peak-hour demands with vehicles and crews that are idle for most of the day. In Washington, D.C., typically only one-third of the buses are used in the midday off-peak period, i.e., two-thirds of the vehicles and two-thirds of the staff have to be idle at that time. The recent introduction of part-time drivers (247, added to a full-time staff of 2,625) has made only a small dent in the problem. Employment of predominantly full-time staff, who are productive only in peak periods, make the peak-period trips more expensive to provide than the off-peak ones. For example, the Sacramento Transit Authority estimated that it costs 80.9¢ per unit to carry passengers in peak periods on its system and only 51.9¢ to carry passengers in off-peak hours. As the same fare is charged throughout the day, the off-peak riders are forced to subsidize the peak-hour ones, which means that the peak-hour services attract more passengers than is good for the health of the franchised operator, while too few passengers are attracted in the off-peak periods. Clearly, any competition by jitneys or shared taxis in the peak periods could help a franchised company by allowing it to reduce its fleet and to use efficiently a greater proportion of its resources consequently being used continuously throughout the day. Thus, it is by no means obvious that informal public transportation, which takes the "cream" of the traffic in the peak periods, would hurt the franchised services. Indeed, as Gilbert Walker pointed out many years ago, in public transport the "cream" is at the bottom of the bottle—there is no money to be made from carrying peak services if the size of the peak-period fleet greatly exceeds the off-peak requirements.

Providing Unprofitable Services

It is in the nature of private enterprise that it provides services for profit and that it does not provide service where there is no profit. If, then, urban public transportation were to be provided by private enterprise, who would provide the unprofitable services? The services on weak routes? Sunday services? "Night owl" services? Peak-hour services? Who would provide transport for school children? For the sick? For the poor?

The answer can once again be—private enterprise. With suitable arrangements, private contractors can carry unprofitable, as well as profitable, services. There are at least two ways of accomplishing this:

User-Side Subsidies. If a community feels that certain groups should travel without having to pay the full cost, they can be given special tickets or vouchers at reduced rates. School children in Washington, D.C., and in many American cities get tokens for which they pay 10¢ each while full-fare riders have to pay 65¢. The tokens are only valid on buses. In some cities, tokens issued to elderly and handicapped people can be used on taxis as well as on buses. The provision of tickets or tokens, like the better-known food stamps, is an example of user-side subsidies. Supplier-side subsidies, on the other hand, involve direct payment to service suppliers such as transit companies. The essence of user-side subsidies is that the user, while being helped by a subsidy, is not confined to any particular supplier, can select the best service for his purposes, and may change to another service at will. Much of the recent information on user-side subsidies is available from demonstration programs financed by UMTA which published detailed reports evidencing positive results. The project in Danville (Ill.), for example, showed that door-to-door taxi service for elderly people was provided at a much lower cost per passenger than was possible by a publicly-operated "dial-a-ride" system and that the impact on the taxi operators, who were the suppliers, was an approximate 15% increase in business. In Seattle, the transit agency has contracts with 29 area cab companies that participate in the city's user-side subsidy program for the elderly and handicapped. Qualified users purchase a $10.00 book of taxicab scrip for $4.00. They may use the scrip with the taxicab company of their choice. The city distributes $55,000 of taxicab scrip per month paid for with coupon revenues, local government funds, and a 10% federal subsidy. The taxicab user subsidy program achieves a good deal of service with a minimum of administrative burden. The Kingston (N.C.) taxicab service for elderly and handicapped persons is also operated with a user-side subsidy. Eligible residents register with the city and receive an identification number and card to be used in purchasing as much as $25.00 worth of rides a month. Participants pay 50% of the face value of the tickets which may be used on any taxicab operating in the city. The city redeems the coupons at face value. Similar user-side subsidy programs are in operation in San Francisco, Arlington (Va.), and Richland (Wash.).

Contract Services. Another way in which private enterprise can be used to provide unprofitable services is to contract out required services to taxi firms, as is now happening in California and elsewhere (pp. 45). Lower subsidies are the case with publicly-operated services as the rule, and there is the added benefit of stimulating a local industry.

Cross-Subsidization—A Practice to be Avoided

Both of the methods described above—user-side subsidies and contract services—involve subsidies paid directly by a community to meet certain social costs. If the elected representatives of a community decide that certain travelers need financial help, it is only proper that they vote funds accordingly. It is, however, quite another matter to finance such services through *cross-subsidization* which involves the provision of some services at excessive profits so that others may be provided at a loss. This practice can be criticized on the following grounds:

- It is undemocratic, in that it gives powers of taxation and subsidy to bodies that are not elected and not equipped to decide who should be

forced to give how much and to whom.
- It prevents the fullest development of the services that earn surpluses because the extra revenues are used to maintain unprofitable services.
- It discourages public transport operators from assessing the expenses and revenues of individual service elements, with a view to changing the fares when called for, expanding profitable services and dropping unprofitable routes and schedules, in that it allows them only to look at their *total* expenses.
- It is an inefficient way of helping those in need, in that many who get the benefits do not really require them.

For these reasons, cross-subsidization cannot be recommended as a method of financing unprofitable services. It cannot survive under competitive conditions, and its demise would do more good than harm to the public transportation industry.

Conclusion
While the U.S. does have some high-quality public transportation services operating without subsidy—shared taxis, subscription services, van pools and jitneys—they are still comparatively few in number and their expansion is restricted by regulatory constraints which have been recognized for many years. Back in 1972, the U.S. Department of Transportation noted that:

> The present regulatory environment in urban public transportation, including obsolete franchise limitations and market-entry barriers for taxicabs and jitneys, restricts the efficient operation of the urban transportation system. The removal of such regulatory constraints is likely to lead to more efficient use of the transportation system and increase the options available to its users.

Long overdue steps that might be taken by all levels of government to remove these constraints are discussed in the final chapter.

5
A Practical Implementation Program

In testimony before the Senate Subcommittee on Intergovernmental Relations in July 1981, C. Kenneth Orski, former Associate Administrator of the Urban Mass Transportation Administration, affirmed that:

> ...transit is in trouble because it has failed to respond to the changing demands of the marketplace. It follows, that its future viability hinges less on what the federal government is going to do than on what happens at the local level. For, if public transportation is to regain some of its lost appeal and utility and become once again economically viable, it must be significantly restructured, both in terms of the type of service it should provide and in terms of who should provide it and who should pay for it.
>
> We stand, I believe, on the brink of a major re-orientation in the way we think about local transportation. Fiscal pressures confronting local government, combined with sharply escalating operating costs and a climate of public disenchantment with regular transit's performance, are prompting local communities to reassess the effectiveness of their current transportation services and to search for more effective and economical alternatives.
>
> The search is leading them away from large, monopolistic, centrally-managed service delivery systems toward approaches characterized by decentralized operation, service diversity, competition, and a sense of shared public/private responsibility for service provision. In sum, we are witnessing nothing less than a fundamental rethinking of the basic premises of public transportation. And while the final outcome of this process cannot be foreseen, there is sufficient evidence to suggest that it will lead to a major restructuring and redefinition of America's local transportation.

It is difficult to better Ken Orski's diagnosis and his prescription for improvement. The problem is how to get from the present situation to the more flexible stage envisaged. Fortunately or unfortunately, in 1982 there is a powerful incentive to change: the decision by the federal government to phase out many of the subsidies for public transportation. This decision is likely to stimulate all those who are interested in introducing self-financing systems to supplement, or even to replace, some of the existing subsidized services.

It is not suggested that the abolition of monopoly franchises would suddenly enable all public transportation to be provided at a profit by small operators in all U.S. cities. As noted before, these "informal" services may only have a support role in some of the major cities, but even this auxiliary function, integrated properly with other transportation systems catering to heavy demand along major corridors, can make a significant contribution to urban mobility and absorb peak-period pressures.

It is essential that local transportation commissions and publicly-owned carriers evidence a change in attitude, as is indeed beginning to happen in a few communities, and consider the private, informal, transport providers not as adversaries but as allies in coping with the problem of moving people quickly, comfortably and economically within metropolitan areas. The most successful informal transportation arrangements where public and private services coexist are those that are fully integrated with the official service providers. Coordinating mechanisms like Knoxville's Transportation Broker, which matches mobility needs with transport suppliers in the best interests of users and the public at large, can help achieve smooth working relationships among all service providers. Local government needs to stand behind such efforts. There are many communities, including those with no bus or train services, where the informal services might be able to carry the whole load. Not only do less developed countries provide a model. The experience of a major capital city—Buenos Aires—provides evidence that an unprofitable public system can operate successfully after being returned to private hands. To provide the climate in which private transportation suppliers can make an optimum contribution to the mobility of our cities, action is urgently required to:

- Remove regulatory obstacles;
- Work out efficient arrangements for insurance;
- Devise equitable methods to charge for shared-taxi services.

Regulatory Obstacles
The main regulatory obstacles are probably the franchising agreements under which local authorities control the entry into the transport business of

potential suppliers and also the fares and conditions of service of established operators. What these restrictions mean in practice is that, for example, the owner of a small taxi firm in Orange County has to negotiate with six local authorities to get permission to improve his services to the public. There is an urgent need to remove many of the powers that government officials have over transport services, powers that do not exist in respect to other services that can be supplied competitively. While the activities of hairdressers, hotel operators, and restaurateurs are subject to inspection by local authorities, an owner wishing to expand services does not need permission from local officials, nor is there control over the charges to the public.

Insurance Coverage

Insurance companies are well organized to provide insurance coverage for individuals driving privately in their own vehicles and for conventional taxicabs and conventional mass transit systems. Insurance is now available for van pool operations, thanks to a scheme worked out by the National Association of Van Pool Operators. However, the small public transport operator—such as a firm leasing buses for subscription services—still has difficulty in getting insurance due, in part, to obscurity in the law. There is also a lack of claims experience for this sort of operation, so the insurance industry finds it difficult to assess the risks. This is clearly a field in which more work needs to be done by the insurance industry, and there might even be a case for government to underwrite some risks until more experience is gained.

Two to three pedicabs a day are now being turned out in Torrance, Ca., to supply a slowly-increasing market along the West Coast. They have appeared in San Diego and moves are afoot to have them circulate in New Orleans' French Quarter. About a hundred of them can be found in Honolulu where enterprising Dan Webber founded Paradise Pedicab in 1977. He is also behind the California manufacturing operation.

Fares for Shared Taxis
The shared taxi mode cannot develop without a simple, acceptable charging scheme, which would serve the interests of both the main parties involved: the suppliers and users of shared taxis. A number of charging schemes were discussed in Chapter 4, but none has gained widespread acceptance or even publicity. Local authorities should encourage taxi firms in their areas to use existing methods for ride-sharing or to devise new ones. New hardware and software, such as shared taxi meters and dispatching systems that are at, or beyond, the prototype stage in Europe and the U.S., should be tested in actual street environments. Local governments should consider contributing or absorbing a portion of the cost of such trial installations in cooperation with taxi firms providing service in their cities. Available technology also permits exterior message boards indicating direction and number of passengers aboard, which would improve speed and convenience by avoiding unnecessary stops.

The Tasks Ahead at Different Government Levels
County and City Tasks. By virtue of their powers to license public services, county and city governments have a key role to play in the development of new public transportation services. Their role should be permissive, i.e., would-be operators of public transport should be allowed to provide services in the same way that would-be shopkeepers are allowed to set up shops. Where public transportation services are considered inadequate, the local authorities could set up "transportation brokers" as in Knoxville and contract for better services by a process of bidding. San Diego deregulated its transport services in 1979 and, in consequence, the numbers of taxicabs operating in the city increased from about 400 to 700 within a period of two years. Jitneys have also tripled, from seven to 25 vehicles over the same period. Seattle has done likewise and the fleet of 355 cabs operating on D-day—de-regulation day—has now grown to more than 500. Each cab operator is allowed to set his own fare structure, but must display it prominently. And in New York, where the number of taxi medallions has been frozen at 11,787 for 40 years, Mayor Koch has appointed a committee to hold hearings on whether and how market forces should be allowed to operate. There will be fireworks for sure because a taxi medallion now changes hands at around $60,000, but a return to the prewar days of free competition may be in the offing.

Tasks at the State Level. State governments have substantial stakes in urban transportation: first, as providers of funds for roads, they have an interest in roads being used efficiently; second, as legislators, they are in a position to influence the licensing regulations passed by local governments; third, in some cases (e.g. Connecticut) they are themselves the licensing authorities for their cities; and, fourth, in some cases (e.g. Maryland, New York, Pennsylvania) they provide substantial financial assistance to urban transport systems. Many states are therefore in a strong position to finance innovation rather than stagnation and to require urban areas to change their policies as a condition for receiving state support. For example, operating subsidies for buses could be made conditional on part-time labor being employed for peak-period services. In some cases (e.g. California) it might be possible, and desirable, for the state to pass laws that would abolish the powers of local authorities to create monopolies for bus and taxi firms.

Tasks at the Federal Level. Although the federal government has no direct responsibility for providing urban transportation services, it has an interest in the provision of high-quality, self-financing services because of its continuing expenditures on transport subsidies. It has already decided to phase out operating subsidies, but continues to offer capital grants—a somewhat illogical position which encourages local operators to skimp on maintenance (which already leaves much to be desired) and pull the stops on capital investment. The Department of Transportation, which has a unique overview of urban transport developments in the U.S. and a good knowledge of developments abroad, could promote the development of high-quality, self-financing public transport services by:

- collecting relevant information on a systematic basis and making it available to lower governmental levels;
- coupling lower grants for capital expenditures with targeted support for innovation, experimentation, research and publicity that will encourage the private sector to take up the slack in the provision of public transportation.

The Contribution of Private Enterprise

While government—at all levels—can assist the re-alignment of public transport by removing the constraints on private enterprise, it is the private sector itself that must take the lead in putting public transportation on a profitable basis. A major role in this process can be played by taxi firms, independent bus operators, and car rental firms. A different role, but also one of major importance, can be played by the transportation consulting profession. For example, some of the cost-saving activities of the Tidewater Transportation District Commission were proposed and carried out by the ATE Management and Service Co., which has transportation management contracts with 51 public systems in the U.S. Its smaller rival, ATC, currently manages 16 systems. These and other firms could form the catalyst for and nucleus of private sector supply of public transportation services if their employers—and cities—allow them to operate in a de-regulated environment. Public interest groups with expertise in tailoring alternative services to the needs of different traveling publics are also in the wings, ready to advise and assist cities in devising systems involving the mix of conventional and informal suppliers that is best suited to local needs. Ken Orski's new Corporation for Public Mobility, which became operational in 1982, has the specific objective of assisting cities to devise innovative, low cost, self-financing solutions to the public transportation crisis.

Transportation is the nerve system of our civilization. Without it we face paralysis. Due to the rising cost of those resources that, in this country at least, have given almost everyone personal mobility, we must devise means to move people more efficiently and economically. The sensitive integration of informal and conventional transportation systems in a de-regulated environment, where the market is allowed to respond to the mobility needs of the traveling public with a bare minimum of assistance or oversight by local government, will go a long way toward meeting this objective. Given a chance, free enterprise transportation could handle an increasing share of the public's transportation requirements.

One of the more than thirty vehicles now participating in San Diego's jitney program: owner-drivers predominate

Annex

Source References

Amos, R.F. "Shared Taxis in Belfast." Presented at the PTRC Summer Annual Meeting, University of Warwick, July 1978.

Barden, S.A., and J.R.V. Seneviratne. "Public Light Bus Operation Survey—1972." Technical Report 115, Traffic and Transport Division, Public Works Department, Hong Kong, 1972.

Barwell, Ian. "The Matatu Public Transport Sector in Nairobi." Report to the World Bank, Urban Projects Department, November 1979.

Baumann, D.M., T. An, and J. Copper. "Automation of Paratransit Fare Computation and Dispatching." Transportation Research Record No. 608, Washington, D.C.: Transportation Research Board, 1976.

Eckert, Ross, and George Hilton. "The Jitneys." *Journal of Law and Economics*. University of Chicago, October 1972.

Government of Singapore, Annual Reports of the Registry of Vehicles.

Grava, Sigurd. "Locally Generated Transportation Modes of the Developing World." *Urban Transportation Economics—Special Report 181*, pp. 84-95. Washington, D.C.: National Academy of Sciences, Transportation Research Board, 1978.

———. "The Jeepneys of Manila." *Traffic Quarterly*, Vol. 26, pp. 465-483, October 1962.

Hilton, George. "Federal Transit Subsidies." Washington, D.C.: American Enterprise Institute, 1974.

Kirby, Ronald F. "Targeting Money Effectively: User-Side Transportation Subsidies." *Journal of Contemporary Studies*, Vol. IV, No. 2, Spring 1981.

———, et al. "Para-Transit—Neglected Options for Urban Mobility." Washington, D.C.: The Urban Institute, 1975.

Lavares, Jose P., Jr. "Jeepney Transport Policy Formulation." Paper presented at World Bank Seminar on Urban Transport, Bangkok, 1980.

Mass Transit (various issues) 555 National Press Building, Washington, D.C.

"Personalized Public Transport in Cities in South East Asia." London: Jamieson Mackay and Partners, March 1979.

Rees, Clarke C. "The Minibuses of Kuala Lumpur." London: Jamieson Mackay and Partners, July 1979.

Rimmer, P.J., and H.W. Dick. "Improving Urban Public Transport in Southeast Asian Cities: Some Reflections on the Conventional and Unconventional Wisdom." Paper presented at World Bank Seminar on Urban Transport, Bangkok, 1980.

Saltzman, A., and R.J. Solomon. "Jitney Operations in the United States." Highway Research Record No. 449. Washington, D.C.: Transportation Research Board, 1973.

Sanli, H. Ibrahim. "Dolmus-Minibus System in Istanbul—A Case-Study in Low Cost Public Transport." Istanbul: Institute of Urbanism, Istanbul Technical University, 1977.

Situma, Ian W. "The 'Matatu' Public Transportation of Nairobi." Report to the Mayor and Council of Nairobi, August 1977.

Tunbridge, R.J., and R.L. Jackson. "The Economics of Stage Carriage Operation by Private Bus and Coach Companies." TRRL Report 952. Crowthorne, U.K.: Transport and Road Research Laboratory, 1980.

Urban Transport News (various issues) 1126 National Press Building, Washington, D.C.

Wallis, Ian P. *Private Bus Operation in Urban Areas–Their Economics and Roles.* Australia: R. Travers Morgan Pty., Ltd., 1979.

Walters, A.A. "Costs and Scale of Bus Services." World Bank Staff Working Paper No. 325. Washington, D.C.: World Bank, 1979.

Wells, John. "An Analysis of Taxicab Operating Characteristics." Bethesda, Maryland: International Taxicab Association, 1975.

Wong, Man-Kit. "Public Light Bus (PLB) 'Maxicab' Operation—An Informal Form of Transport." Paper presented at World Bank Seminar on Urban Transport, Bangkok, 1980.

Zahavi, Yacov. "Travel Regularities in Baltimore, Washington, London and Reading." Technical Memorandum attached to Progress Report No. 8 on the UMOT Travel Model II, presented to the U.S. Department of Transportation, Research and Special Programs Administration, Washington, D.C., December 1981.

Shared Ride Policy Statement

To conserve energy, increase productivity and provide an alternative to the exclusive ride taxi service, the International Taxicab Association hereby states its approval and encouragement of the adoption of shared ride taxi principles to all localities where they are not already present.

The ITA proposes a massive effort, both to comply with the federal requirements of having shared ride service available as a precursor of reduced fuel taxes, but also as a recognition of the fact that there are a significant number of potential customers that may be priced out of the traditional exclusive ride taxicab market.

In many locations, regulatory change is required in order to allow taxicab operators to provide these alternative services as part of public transportation and a concerted effort of the members of ITA to move for these changes is also hereby acknowledged, and encouraged.

Basic Principles of Shared Ride

No shared ride customer shall be charged more than an exclusive ride customer for the same trip. The shared ride trip may be provided at a reduced level of service in terms of the total trip time as measured in terms of possible time delays in either access of trip deviation.

All shared ride operations shall emphasize door-to-door, individualized service and security and safety efforts. Extra training of personnel in providing for customer safeguards should accompany each new shared ride service to offset any potential increase in in-vehicle crime or public harassment that might accompany a change to shared ride service.

Each ITA member or group of members who accomplishes the change into a working shared ride regulatory environment shall assist neighboring taxi and paratransit companies by providing information and encouragement to neighboring communities also attempting to change to shared ride service. Extra effort shall be undertaken on the part of each shared ride operator to document improvements of efficiency and to make the public aware of the goals of increased productivity.

Ordinances

Extract from Chapter 28 of Chicago Municipal Code, as amended on December 20, 1979

28-29. Not more than six passengers shall be accepted for transport at one time on any trip in a taxicab: provided that additional passengers under the age of twelve years accompanied by an adult passenger shall be accepted if the taxicab has seating capacity for them.

28-29.1. Group, shared or multiple riding is prohibited in taxicabs except as follows:

(a) The passenger first hiring the taxicab may direct that he be carried exclusively or as part of a group, multiple or shared ride;

(b) The Commissioner, by regulation or rule, may designate certain places where group riding (more than one person entering at the same point and disembarking at one point) or multiple riding (more than one person entering the taxicab at the same point and disembarking at more than one point) is permissible at all times or at certain specified times and may specify the manner of charging for such trips;

(c) The Commissioner, by regulation or rule, may designate certain specified times when group, multiple or shared riding (more than one person entering the taxicab at one or more points and disembarking at one or more points) is permissible and may specify the manner of charging for such trips;

(d) The Commissioner, by regulation or rule, may designate that group riding, multiple riding or shared riding is permissible in the transportation of passengers with an affinity among them, which affinity shall be as defined in such regulation or rule, and may specify the manner of charging for such trips.

Extract from Taxicab Ordinance for the City of Knoxville, Tennessee. Adopted March 22, 1977.

39-600. *Ride Sharing*. It shall be the public policy to encourage and permit ride sharing to increase taxicab efficiency and to reduce the cost of taxicab operations in terms of the cost per passenger. However, the route of the taxicab shall not deviate into more than one additional zone for the purpose of picking up a subsequent passenger. Also, a passenger shall not be required to pay an additional fare resulting from the deviation of the taxicab into an additional zone for the purpose of picking up a subsequent passenger.

39-601. *Public Contract Services.* Holders of certificates of public convenience and necessity to whom contracts for service have been awarded by the Department of Public Transportation Services shall perform such work as specified in such contracts including but not limited to feeder service to and from fixed route buses either publicly or privately owned, feeder service to or from commuter buses either publicly or privately owned, services for the elderly and the handicapped and services for social agencies.

Ride sharing and/or group riding within the limits of the taxicab, as set forth in the certificate of convenience and necessity, shall be allowed in contract services without permission of any of the passengers.

No charges shall be made to passengers for contract service except as provided for in the contract with the City for such services.

Index

Amman 19
Australia 31-33

Bakassi 3, 23
Baltimore 39
Bangkok 30, 31, 38
Belfast 3, 25-26
Black Taxis 3, 25-26
Buenos Aires 2, 11-13, 34, 36, 53, 60

Cairo 2, 19-20
Calcutta 13, 14, 36, 53
Caracas 27, 38
car pools 41, 48
colectivo 11
COM-BUS 47
contract services 6, 45-47, 57
cross subsidization 4, 37, 43, 52, 54, 57-58

Dolmus 2, 17-19

Empresa 12, 13

fare fixing 5, 60, 62
Fine Grid scheme 43, 44

Hong Kong 1, 7, 8, 9, 10, 11, 28, 36
Honolulu 42, 16

insurance 6, 25, 47, 50, 60-61
Istanbul 2, 17-19

Jeepneys 2, 14-17
Jitneys 19-20, 43, 51-53, 58, 62

Khartoum 3, 23
Knoxville (TN) 45, 60, 62
Kuala Lumpur 1, 9, 10, 11

Manila 2, 14-17, 36, 53
Matatu 2, 22-23, 24
Maxicabs 9
Meriden (CT) 5, 43-44
Minibus 2, 6, 7, 9, 10, 13, 17-19, 22, 41, 45, 48

Nairobi 2, 22-23, 24, 37
New Jersey 49-50, 53-54
Norfolk (VA) 45-47
Orski, Kenneth 59-60, 64

Pak Pais 7
part-time 56, 62
passenger miles 10, 13, 50
pedicabs 27, 42, 61
Phoenix (AZ) 5
Pittsburgh (PA) 5
Por Puestos 27, 38
Public Light Buses 8, 9, 10, 28
Publicos 3, 24, 26-27
Puerto Rico 3, 24, 26-27, 32

Ride Shared Vehicle Paratransit 43, 44-45
Route Associations 2, 3, 5, 12, 13, 14, 29, 36, 53-54

Saint Louis (MO) 51-52
Saint Paul (MN) 46-48
San Diego 4, 53, 61, 62, 64
school buses 2, 20-22
Service Cars 51-52
Shared Taxis 5, 6, 18, 18, 25-26, 38, 41
Sherut 19
Singapore 2, 20-22, 28
Subscription Services 5, 20-21, 41, 47, 58, 61

Transportation Broker 45, 60, 62

United Kingdom 3, 25-26, 30, 35, 55
user-side subsidies 56-57

van pools 5, 41, 46, 48-50, 58, 61

Washington, D.C. 4, 29, 36, 41, 42-43, 44, 55, 56
weak routes 4, 54, 56-57

71

The Council for International Urban Liaison (CIUL) was formed in 1976 by the principal local government associations of the U.S. and Canada to promote the international exchange of practical experience in dealing with common urban problems. The Council publishes periodicals and case studies to keep urban policy makers and practitioners abreast of trends and innovations abroad that can help American communities improve the quality of urban life and the effectiveness of local government service delivery. **Urban Innovation Abroad** (monthly) and **Urban Transportation Abroad** (quarterly) are the vehicles of this effort available as a service package at $36 annually. A separate periodical, **The Urban Edge**, is supported by the World Bank as an appropriate technology clearinghouse for professionals with urban concerns in developing nations. Other activities include the organization of workshops, seminars, and study trips to exchange experience on issues of priority concern to local government associations in North America. Policy direction is provided the Council by its constituent local government associations, whose executive directors comprise its Board of Trustees. Financial support comes from foundations, government and industry contracts and service fees. The Council for International Urban Liaison is a non-profit, tax-exempt institution.

For additional information contact: The Council for International Urban Liaison, 818 18th Street, N.W., Washington, D.C. 20006. Telephone: (202)223-1434. John Garvey, Jr., President. George G. Wynne, Director of Communications.

The Institute for Environmental Action is a non-profit organization formed in 1973 in New York City by an international group of urban strategists and environmental activists committed to improving the quality of the built environment. The Institute provides *Direct Assistance in Urban Problem-Solving* and does *Research and Communication* on various urban and environmental issues. Extensive on-site investigation and appraisal of planning, design, development and management issues have been translated into books, reports, exhibits and films. These materials are aimed at promoting an exchange of information on urban environmental improvements among American cities, and between the U.S. and Europe. Among the Institute's current publications are the **Learning From the U.S.A.** series of handbooks on urban improvements in selected American cities, available through a $24 subscription for four volumes. Through **Metropolis**, its offshoot division, the Institute also provides architectural and urban design services to municipalities, community organizations and private developers in the United States, Europe and Latin America.

For additional information contact: The Institute for Environmental Action, 530 West 25th Street, New York, N.Y. 10001. Telephone: (212)620-9773. Roberto Brambilla and Gianni Longo, Directors.